The

You

2004 POETRY

ONCE UPON A RHYME

IMAGINATION FOR
A NEW GENERATION

Co Armagh
Edited by Steph Park-Pirie

 Young**Writers**

First published in Great Britain in 2004 by:
Young Writers
Remus House
Coltsfoot Drive
Peterborough
PE2 9JX
Telephone: 01733 890066
Website: www.youngwriters.co.uk

SB ISBN 1 84460 476 4

Foreword

Young Writers was established in 1991 and has been passionately devoted to the promotion of reading and writing in children and young adults ever since. The quest continues today. Young Writers remains as committed to engendering the fostering of burgeoning poetic and literary talent as ever.

This year's Young Writers competition has proven as vibrant and dynamic as ever and we are delighted to present a showcase of the best poetry from across the UK. Each poem has been carefully selected from a wealth of *Once Upon A Rhyme* entries before ultimately being published in this, our twelfth primary school poetry series.

Once again, we have been supremely impressed by the overall high quality of the entries we have received. The imagination, energy and creativity which has gone into each young writer's entry made choosing the best poems a challenging and often difficult but ultimately hugely rewarding task - the general high standard of the work submitted amply vindicating this opportunity to bring their poetry to a larger appreciative audience.

We sincerely hope you are pleased with our final selection and that you will enjoy *Once Upon A Rhyme Co Armagh* for many years to come.

Contents

John Moore (9)	40
Andrew Daly (10)	40
Jason Lamont (8)	40
Hannah Whittaker (8)	41
Jordan Gibson (8)	41
Nicole Mount (9)	42
Sophie Fleming (9)	42
James Hall (9)	42

Edenderry Primary School

Hayley Johnston (9)	43
Megan Robinson (8)	43
Jordan Deering (8)	44
Hannah Lyttle (7)	44
Lucy Daly (7)	44
Patrick Ortega (7)	45
Rebecca Roberts (8)	45
Victoria Argue (10)	45
Alexander Hawthorne (9)	46
Andrew Steele (10)	46
Jade Megaw (9)	46
Kirsty Burns (9)	47
Darren Leckey (10)	47

Maghaberry Primary School

Robyn-Dee Herdman (10)	48
Colin Tinsley (10)	49

St John's Primary School, Middletown

Carrie Mallon (11)	49
Paschal Carvill (11)	49
Plunkett Hart (11)	50
Barry Trainor (10)	50
Karen McCann (10)	51
Keith Moran (11)	51
Shauna Mooney (10)	52
Kerri McQuaid (10)	52
Orlagh Curry (11)	53
Louise McGuigan (10)	53
Aoife O'Hagan (11)	54
Catherine Spottiswood (10)	54

Jade Hegarty (10)	55
Andrea Shine (11)	55
Philip Sherry (11)	56
Cathal Harnett (11)	56

St Malachy's Primary School, Armagh

Sinead Gillen (10)	57
John Maguire (9)	57
Fionnuala McKenna (10)	58
Nola Boylan (9)	59
Luke Grimley (9)	60
Karen Traynor (10)	61
Carreann Nugent (9)	62
Tiernan Leonard (9)	63
Stephen King (10)	64
Bronagh Grimley (10)	65
Zoe McGirr (10)	66
Rebecca O'Reilly (10)	67
April Flynn (9)	68
Connor Traynor (9)	68
Deirdre O'Reilly (10)	69
Martyn Kenny (9)	70
Tara Kelly (9)	70

St Patrick's Primary School, Armagh

Larisa Gribben (11)	71
Aaron Hannon (10)	71
Michael McCartney (10)	72
Ruairi O'Kane (10)	72
Rory Howard (11)	73
Naomi Campbell (11)	73
Dearbhla Murphy (10)	74
Shane Mallon (11)	74
Lisa Crossen (9)	74
Nathan Young (10)	75
Cailin Kennedy (10)	75
Shay McGahan (11)	75
Lauren Guy (8)	76
Rebecca McGeary (9)	76
Aidan Campbell (9)	76
Kevin McAleavey (8)	77

Natalie Malone (9)	77
Kevin Aherne (8)	78
Jack Hughes (9)	78
Mark Murphy (8)	78
Sean Perry (9)	79
Johnny Bergin (8)	79
Hollie Johnston (9)	80
Cailin McGeown (9)	80
Edel Donnelly (9)	81
Sean O'Neill (8)	81
Aisling White (7)	82
Lauren Mackle (8)	82
Matthew Rice (9)	82
Jack Terrins-Baker (9)	83
Nicole Connolly (9)	83
Emma Toal (8)	84
Joshua Loughran (9)	84
Luke McSherry (9)	85
Ciaran Duffy (9)	85
Damien Gorman (9)	86
Lauren McMahon (7)	87
Niall McCoy (9)	87
Niamh McKee (8)	88
Hannah Pearson (8)	88
Shea McCartney (7)	89
Natasha Murphy (8)	89
Rachel Devlin (8)	89
Conal Baxter (8)	90
Shauna Wilson (7)	90
Ben Lavery (7)	90
Claire Hamilton (8)	91
James Devlin (11)	91
Jane Toner (8)	92
Hannah McCann (8)	92
Cathal McArdle (11)	93
Lauren Pattison (8)	93
Niamh McMahon (10)	94
Nicole Mallon (11)	95
Declan Donnelly (10)	95
Sophie Knipe (11)	95
Lauren Devlin (10)	96
Nicole Reilly (11)	96

Aoife McVeigh (11)	97
Shannon McKeown (11)	97
Niamh Cauldwell (8)	98
Tiarnan McArdle (8)	98
Chloe Mulholland (11)	99
Maria McGee (8)	99
Shannagh Skipsey (8)	99

St Patrick's Primary School, Lurgan

Maeve Mulholland (8)	100
Nuala McMahon (7)	100
Niall McDowell (7)	101
Ciáran Coleman (8)	101
Niall Kerr (8)	101
Ciara Corrigan (7)	102
Tony Mulligan (8)	102

St Teresa's Primary School, Mountnorris

Claire McCone (9)	103
Tracey McSherry (8)	103
Natasha Hamilton (9)	104
Gareth Feenan (10)	104
Brendan O'Hare (7)	104
Tanith Nesbitt (9)	105
Julie McSherry (8)	105
Seamus Toher (11)	106
Zoe Carr (9)	106
Lauren O'Hare (9)	107

Seagoe Primary School

Conan Hoey (9)	107
Shannon Cambell (10)	108
Linzi Maxwell (9)	108
Zoe Hagan (10)	108
Holly Rathore (9)	109
Jason Webb (10)	109
Jessica Gilpin (10)	110
Jonathan Beattie (10)	110
Katy McComb (9)	110
Serena Christie (9)	111

Esther Hewitt (9)	111
Jordan Ritchie (9)	111
Hannah Forsythe (10)	112
Hayley Cullen (9)	112
Michael Busby (10)	112
Richard Carson (10)	113
Lauren Anderson (10)	113
Mark Scott (9)	113
David Busby (10)	114
Lindsey Stevenson (10)	114
Rhys Harris (10)	114
Beth Wright (9)	115
Christine Bell (9)	115
Hannah Todd (9)	115
Jonathan Hilliard (11)	116
Lily Robinson (9)	116
Sarah Clifford (10)	117
Gillian Bell (11)	117
Rebekah Wallace (11)	118

The Armstrong Primary School

Kirsten Doran (7)	118
Rebecca Loney (8)	119
Chloe Wilson (7)	119
Nathan Beatty (8)	120
Matthew Blair (7)	120
Clive Knipe (8)	121
Philip Gordon (8)	121
Cara Best (8)	121
Jessie Kwok (7)	122
Alan Humphries (7)	122
Jason Burt (8)	123
Laura Isted (7)	123
Hannah McClure (7)	123
Lisa Murray (8)	124
Madeleine Armstrong (8)	124
Robert Armstrong (9)	124
Stephanie Chan (10)	125
Robert Davidson (8)	125
James Neville (10)	125

Claire Gilmore (10)	126
Ashleigh Kerr (9)	126
Emily Colvin (10)	126
Kelly McNeilly (10)	127
Timmy Hassard (9)	127
Alice Bingham (10)	127
Ethan Ross (8)	128
Lindsey Smyth (9)	128
Dean Symington (9)	129
Emma Blaney (9)	129
Kerry-Anne Wright (9)	130
Rosalind McClean (8)	130
Kylie Tucker (8)	130
Scott Armstrong (8)	131
Hannah McCann (9)	131
Michael Hoey (9)	132
Sarah Stewart (8)	132
Michael Dobbs (9)	132
Danielle Sutcliffe (9)	133
Jane Oliver (8)	133
Josh Finlay (10)	133
Simon Watson (7)	134
Emma McNeilly (7)	134
Adam Marshall (7)	134
Christopher Gillespie (8)	135
Ellen Donaldson (8)	135
Claire Hanna (8)	136
William Gillanders (8)	136
Sophie Gillespie (8)	137

The Cope Primary School

Ellen Coulter (10)	137
Rebecca Reid (8)	137
James Hewitt (10)	138
Jenny Blevins (11)	138
Richard Allen (11)	138
Stephen Hook (10)	139
Lee Coleman (10)	139
David McKennell (11)	139
Christine Crawford (11)	140

Anna Ritchie (10)	141
Leah Ewart (10)	141
Natasha Frizzell (11)	142
Lynsey Browne (10)	142
Judith Topley (8)	143
Matthew Hooks (8)	143
Leanne Wilson (8)	143
Emma Kane (8)	144
Laura Hewitt (8)	144
Matthew Irwin (7)	144
Kerri Hewitt (8)	145
Jonathan Hewitt (8)	145
Edith Henry (7)	145
Megan Frizzell (7)	146
Simon Emerson (8)	146
Jemma McHugh (7)	146
Alex Henderson (8)	147
Alistair Scott (8)	147
Samantha Cummings (7)	147
Aaron Winter (8)	148
Adam West (11)	148
Rosie Armstrong (7)	149
Alana McMinn (9)	149
Abigail Duke (10)	149
Claire Martin (9)	150
Lynn Brownlee (10)	150
Keith Walker (9)	150
Jennifer West (10)	151
Mark Lavery (9)	151
Julie Kane (10)	151
Emma Allen (9)	152
Stuart Walker (9)	152
Hazel Irwin (10)	152
Roger Allen (9)	153
Neill Buckley (9)	153
Rachel McKinney (10)	153
James Scott (9)	154
Megan Emerson (10)	154
Lewis Forsythe (10)	155
Gareth Strain (10)	155
David Bell (10)	155

The Poems

My Alien

T he alien came on Friday teatime
H e knocked on the door and said 'Hello'
E ager as he was he didn't eat a thing

A blaze went his sneeze, burning up
L anded in Lurgan and came to stay
 I cy cold were his feet, from an igloo he came
E ats up all the eggs
N ever knew a nest from a newspaper

A t eight o'clock we went to bed
T he little sneak ate all the cocoa

H amburgers, everything was gone
O h if I could get that alien
M y hands would go round his neck
E arly next morning, I woke up, and it was all a dream.

Christian Cowan (8)
Annaghmore Primary School

The Family Talk

My dad is great
He is strong
My mum is big
She is not a great cook at home
But she is mad!
My brother is silly at times
And he is small,
My sister is a good girl,
But sometimes bad!

My mum wants to go to Florida,
My dad wants to go to Russia
My brother wants to go to America
And my sister wants to go to Africa,
To see all the wild animals.

Andrew Trueman (8)
Annaghmore Primary School

If You Want To See Animals

If you want to see a tiger
You must go down to the wet, grassy
Middle of the Australian jungle
I know a tiger who's living down there
Yes, if you want to see a tiger
You must go down to the wet, grassy
Middle of the Australian jungle.
You must go down and say
Terrific tiger
Terrific tiger
Terrific t . . . iger
And out she'll pounce
But don't stand there
Run for your life!

If you want to see a crocodile
You must go down to the muddy, slushy
Middle of the Asian river
I know a crocodile who's living in there
Yes, if you want to see a crocodile
You must go down to the muddy, slushy
Middle of the Asian river
You must go down and say
Snappy croc
Snappy croc
Snappy crooooooooooooc
And out she'll pop
But don't just stand there
Run for your life!

Stephanie Ashfield-Beattie (8)
Annaghmore Primary School

If You Want To See A Monster

If you want to see a monster
You must go up to Monster hill,
It's smelly, muddy, slippery and horrible.

I know a monster who lives up there
She is green with red spots,
She has four eyes, two mouths, six ears and two noses,
She is nasty fierce, and eats teachers.

Yes if you want to see a monster you must go
Up to Monster hill.

Go up quietly and say
Come out monster, who eats teachers
Come out monster, who eats teachers
Come out monster, who eats teacherrrsss.

And out she'll jump
But don't just stick around
'Run for your life'
Especially if you're a teacher.

Samantha Richardson (8)
Annaghmore Primary School

An Animal Alliteration Poem

One obnoxious orang-utan going out of the ozone layer
Two thankful tortoises trading toxic tonics
Three tropical toads tugging tunics
Four faithful flatfish, fitting frameworks
Five friendly frogs, frying fundamental fudge
Six septic slime monsters surviving in the sewer
Seven shameful self employed shellfish
Eight eager earwigs, enjoying Easter
Nine naughty newts nibbling on nuts
Ten traditional trolls making trillions.

Adam Greenaway (9)
Annaghmore Primary School

Cats

I thought cats were fluffy
But when I got home from school
It had left a rat sitting outside
Our door on the mat.

He didn't even want it
He had just left it dead on the mat.
My dad said, 'I told you not to get a cat
Just look!'

He has left blood on the mat
The cat should have just eaten it
Somewhere else.
I am very cross because
He left a rat on the mat!

He is going to have to eat it
Because he is so bad
Just look at that mat.

Clarissa Hewitt (7)
Annaghmore Primary School

Summer

S ummer is a time when the sky turns red afar
U nder a palm tree looking at the stars
M urmuring the moon is too bright
M um says it's like a night light
E verlasting sun that can never go down until sunset
R emember to wear suncream or you'll get sunburnt I bet.

T he waves are calm and still
I n time I've seen a wave as huge as a hill
M ore leaves are falling now that's bad,
E ntering the autumn, is really sad.

Michelle Burns (9)
Annaghmore Primary School

Butterfly Butterfly

Butterfly, butterfly, fly through the air.
Butterfly, butterfly, you fly so sweetly.
Butterfly, butterfly, come to me.
Butterfly, butterfly, wings so colourful.
Butterfly, butterfly, wings so old.
You fly through the grass like a bird.
You fly through the sky like a big dragonfly
But don't let that bad, bad owl
Eat you up or go gobble, gobble, gobble.
You make nature a wonderful thing
A whole crowd of butterflies are flying in the air
To make nature wonderful.
The colour of your wings are pink, green, red and orange
These are wonderful colours.
I will always admire butterflies,
And how you fly like a dragonfly.

Jonathan Small (7)
Annaghmore Primary School

Nature

Nature is a butterfly through the sky
Butterflies flutter in the air.

Birds are looking for worms for their baby chicks.

The wind is blowing the leaves off the trees
And the leaves are on the ground.

Flowers bloom in the spring
And the bees come out.

The lambs are pouncing around in the fields.

Daffodils blow in the wind.

Amy Boyd (7)
Annaghmore Primary School

My Old Dog

My old dog is a faithful old dog
He takes great care of me
He washes my face with his tongue
And climbs all over my knee.

He wakes me in the morning
And wakes me in the night
And dear help the postman
He gives him such a fright.

He dirtys my house
He eats my shoes
He makes such mess
And won't let my mummy watch the news.

He rips holes in the carpet
And puddles on the floor
Pulls up the plants
And scrapes at the door.

He really is a treasure
A real sight to see
But don't go too close
Or you'll go home with a flea.

Andrew Johnston (7)
Bleary Primary School

The Spaceship

The spaceship was in the sky
When I saw it flying by
The aliens waved hello
One was green and one was yellow
A really strange looking fellow
The aliens looked funny
But then it was sunny
And I could not see very well
Now it's not cool to tell.

Aaron Wylie (8)
Bleary Primary School

Young Writers - Once Upon A Rhyme Co Armagh

Sweets

I like sweets, it is a special treat
It is even better than roast meat
Hard and soft, crunchy and smooth
I like it when they stick to my tooth.

I like chocolate, so does my mummy
It's even better when it's in my tummy
Easter eggs I like the most
Better than jam on my toast.

Fruitella are my favourite sweets
I like them better than breakfast wheats
Chewing gum is really cool
We are not allowed to eat it in school.

Every six months I go for a check-up
And the dentist gives them a clean-up.
She tells me sweets are bad for my teeth
That really fills me full of grief.

Chloe Douglas (7)
Bleary Primary School

Go On Holiday

Go on holiday
on the first of May.

Go on a plane,
to Spain.
It's such a pain
to leave the rain!

The golden sun shines,
as the people bob in lines,
on the bright blue sea
for all to see.

Get on a plane I can't wait,
I sure won't be late.

Rachel Slack (7)
Bleary Primary School

Winter

Robins flying in the air
Flying high without a care
Snowdrops coming from the ground
Baby hedgehogs never found
White cats hidden beneath the snow
Farmers feed gets very low
Night is coming very quick
People getting very sick
Birds are going to migrate
Animals go to hibernate
Floods are rising very high
Birds are singing in the sky
Winter's going far away
It shall come another day.

Naomi Nelson (8)
Bleary Primary School

I Saw A Fairy

At the bottom of my garden
I believe I saw a fairy
She was very small and cute
And not at all scary.

She was all in pink
With a little lovely dress
Not at all like me
I was all in a mess.

I tried to sneak closer
On this beautiful day
But I gave her a fright
And she flew away.

Jessica McKitterick (7)
Bleary Primary School

The Moon

The moon
Hangs suspended
In the sky,
Like . . .
A large, gold medal,
A giant, yellow frisbee,
A Jacob's water biscuit,
A Cheese 'n' Onion Frisp,
An enormous melon.
It travels . . .
Across the pale night sky,
Between the stars,
Around the Earth
It shines . . .
A gleaming light
Keeping us safe
Showing us the way
Making a silver river
On the dark lake
It fades . . .
Away
As the sun rises
But winks
Because at night it will be back!

Jessica Wilson (7)
Bleary Primary School

Bumblebees

Bumblebees are funny things
They fly along on tiny wings
They visit lots of pretty flowers
And buzz around for hours and hours.

They live in hives with other bees
Underground or up in trees.
They spend their time making honey,
For baby bees who think it's yummy.

The one in charge is called the Queen
She stays inside and isn't seen.
She will not sting if you say please,
But have you ever seen her knees?

The bumblebee is very shy,
It's shyer than the butterfly.
It doesn't mind if you just watch it,
But you should never try to catch it.

John Uprichard (8)
Bleary Primary School

My Cat

My cat is as tall as a tree.
He sleeps in an enormous basket with a
little toy bee.
He even eats dog food and Sunday dinner too.
My cat climbs on the mantelpiece and
knocks down all the candles and ornaments.
He even bites the postman and the milkman.
My cat is exasperating
I hate my cat!

Jessica Gracey (7)
Bleary Primary School

Baby Brothers

Baby brothers can be fun,
But after a while they'll make your eyes run.

They don't even sleep right,
Because they'll always wake you in the night.

They will *always* be happy,
After they do something in their nappy.

They'll pull your hair,
Sometimes they're worse than a nightmare.

Sometimes you'll wonder why,
'Why, oh why do you have to cry?'

Well, I have to admit they can be funny,
Cute, cuddly, and as sweet as honey!

Catherine Dynes (10)
Bleary Primary School

My Dog

My dog is so funny
He acts like a bunny
He plays with stones
And thinks they are bones
He is a fool
And likes to drool
He likes to play ball
And is very tall
He runs like mad
And is very bad
He doesn't like visitors
And thinks they are prisoners
That's my dog Yogi
And I love him.

Mark Conn (10)
Bleary Primary School

The Cartoon Party

I was invited to a cartoon party
Everyone was there
From Angelica out of the Rugrats
To Yogi the cartoon bear.

Oh look there's Bart and Homer Simpson
Of course there's Scooby Doo
Don't forget Tom and Jerry
Eeyore and Tigger too.

Now who else was there, oh yes,
Pluto and Mickey Mouse
Nemo the little clownfish
And Bear from the Big Blue House.

I really can't mention the rest
Cos Mum made me go to bed
I wish there was no such thing as school
And it was always a party instead.

David Harrison (9)
Bleary Primary School

Teachers

They drive into school
They think they are cool
With their make-up and all,
Get to work they call,
Do your work or you'll get it all wrong,
She calls the roll, 'Timmy Greg'
'Miss he's sick today.'
'I saw him just out there, I don't think he cares.'
'There's only one child here,'
'Yes Miss it's me.'
'Yes,' said Miss and she jumped with glee.

Matthew Wright (8)
Bleary Primary School

My Puppy

My puppy is short and thin
Even though he eats potato skins
He can be funny at times
When he's running about with the Portadown Times.
On my brother's wooden floor
He skips and skids beside the door.
He has a course around the chairs
When the family is eating chocolate eclairs
At the weekend he goes mad
With his friends that are glad
When he's having an afternoon bath
We all laugh
'Cause he splashes water on the floor
We always run for the door.
If we lost him we would be sad
Because we know he's a good little lad.

Philip Davison (10)
Bleary Primary School

Snowy My Rabbit

Snowy is so cool
He does not drool
He pops his head out of a box
And he is like a little ox
He has a friend cat
Called Sophie, lies on a mat
He throws toys up in the air
And sometimes I'll bring him to a fair
My granny thinks I should enter him in
a show
And if he wins he'll get a bow
He is as white as snow
And hates to get out when the wind
starts to blow.

Fiona Kelly (10)
Bleary Primary School

The Rabbit

The rabbit sits in her run
Her loppy ears blow in the wind.
She nibbles a carrot,
That lies in the grass.
She runs into her bed,
It is nice and warm inside.
Her water bottle goes drip, drip, drip.
A dog starts to bark!
She gets up fast to listen,
Her ears prick up.
She walks over slowly to her food bowl,
And she eats some bunnymunch.
She sleeps well that night,
In her warm comfy bedroom.
And in the morning she gets up again,
And gets let out.
She eats a new carrot,
Very quietly she nibbles.
And now she is so quiet,
You cannot hear her nibble.

Aaron McCormick (10)
Bleary Primary School

Homework

Homework can be so boring
Adding and subtracting
Why can't my teacher stop selecting
Maths, English all that stuff
I think she is being a little too rough
Five days a week I suffer
Homework is getting even tougher
I'm tired of all this homework
More boring every night
Besides I know I'm right.

Victoria Laird (11)
Bleary Primary School

The Zoo

I went to the zoo one fine sunny day,
And started to watch the animals play.
There were elephants, giraffes and hippos too,
But my favourite was the kangaroo.

I liked to watch the monkeys swinging from tree to
tree,
While the hyenas sat and laughed with glee.
We ate our picnic by the lake,
But the flamingos came to eat my cake.

The sun was setting in the sky,
Which meant I had to say goodbye.
I really enjoyed my trip to the zoo,
But it's back to the country to hear the cows moo!

Laura Russell (11)
Bleary Primary School

Dreams

I dreamt last night
Of a wonderful place
Where the sun was shining bright
The birds were singing cheerfully
High up in the trees above
The lazy stream flowed slowly by
As the fish jumped towards the sky.

On a grassy hill not far away
I saw a newborn fawn
Nibbling on tufts of grass
As his mother watched closely by
And just then I woke up
My wonderful dream was over.

Laura Gordon (10)
Bleary Primary School

The Popular One

There's a girl at our school,
Who's a real hit with the boys
And she treats all of us,
Like we're her little toys.

She goes around in her pink skirt,
Pretending that she's the best.
But I really think she's a show off,
And so does all of the rest.

She goes around shopping,
Flashing her credit card around.
And cries in her sweet little voice
'Oh look at these shoes I've found.'

She's always been queen of mean,
I really have to say.
But I'd better stop talking about her,
'Cause look! She's coming our way.

Rebecca Murphy (10)
Bleary Primary School

I Love Foals

I love foals the way they drink the way they eat
It's lovely to see a newborn foal
With its little fluffy tail and its little black mane
I love to see the foals first time out of the stable
They put their front feet here and their back feet there
And they think it's just great
Then when they're put into the field all you hear is neigh, neigh,
neigh
Then when it is time to take them in, no smile on its face
But I still love him I think he's kinda cute
That's the life of my foal.

Lawson McKitterick (10)
Bleary Primary School

Shoes!

Shoes! Oh shoes! I love you so much
So many sizes so many to choose
Size and colour I can't decide
The size of heel, short or tall, stout or narrow
Square toed I just don't know.

Each pair for a job that has to be done
I know my favourite for each one
Pink with black trousers are fab
Blue trainers for school they aren't so bad
Easy to wear easy to clean
Just stuff them in the washing machine.

Laces and buckles are not the best
But velcro gets it done in less
At first it's hard but when we learn
Laces can be so much fun
Why did we worry I just don't know
We need not to worry just enjoy
Step out together
Shoes! Oh shoes! I love you so much.

Catherine Bell (11)
Bleary Primary School

Teachers

Teachers are smart
Teachers are weird
Some teachers have long hairy beards
Some teachers put on too much make-up
And look like a clown
Some other teachers are great and should wear
A crown.
Some other teachers laugh like a pig
Others go round school wearing wigs
As for others they would act like children
And would go wild.

Charlotte McCully (9)
Bleary Primary School

I See . . .

I see around me many fields of green
I see blue oceans and crystal clear
streams
I see skies full of fluffy white clouds
I see birds that sing aloud.

I see the sea so clear and blue
I see the grass in the morning dew
I see robins dancing in the grass
I see seagulls gliding as they pass.

I see people walking dogs
I see a fire that's full of logs
I see Dad watching TV
I see Mum making tea.

I see my favourite lollipop lady
I see her stopping cars for a baby
I see my teacher drinking tea
I see our friends waiting for you and
me.

Christopher Calvert (10)
Bleary Primary School

My Sister

My sister can't stop singing
Her clothes look minging
She puts her hair in different ways
Her friends come round and never stay
But now she is coming sixteen
She may be not as mean.
I hope and pray she'll go away
And only visit on Bank Holidays.

Benjamin McCully (8)
Bleary Primary School

My Pets

I have a kangaroo
And a cat called Boo
I have a shark called Bites
But he gives me a fright
I have a chinchilla
And she's called Cilla
But the kangaroo is a bit of a riot
He's always jumping about and he won't
Keep quiet
And Boo she's never off the loo
I think it's what we're feeding her
Mum thinks so too.
The shark called Bites can't get enough to eat
But he only likes meat
But Cilla the chinchilla isn't too bad
Bet she thinks the rest are barking mad!

Rebecca Wylie (10)
Bleary Primary School

My MG Car

A MG is so cool,
It really does rule,
It is a sporty car,
Not a dopey car,
It is a small but very fast car,
A bright yellow flying machine,
With a nice sound from the engine
Which goes voom voom,
Very shiny wheels but not a lot of room,
It glides along the road like an aeroplane,
And people stop and stare,
I feel like I'm king of the road,
With leather seats to sit on,
And the wind blows through my hair,
When I'm driving in my MG car.

Ryan Hill (9)
Bleary Primary School

My Dog

My dog is so cool,
He is a super dude,
He chases a frisbee
And it is really crispy.
His name is Glenn,
And I think he is a plane,
He splashes in puddles,
Until he's soaking wet,
He runs like a wild cat,
And if he saw one,
He would fly like a scary bat.
He is so funny,
He acts like a bunny,
From his cage of my shed,
He is like ice,
And now he acts like a fool,
And he chases the hens,
In the garden he is so cool,
He acts like a fool.
He chases my friend,
She is lovely,
He can jump as high,
As a kangaroo!

Paula McKitterick (8)
Bleary Primary School

Dogs

My dog is so cool
Even though she is a fool.

She is so small and cuddly too
But I love her as much as you

When I come home
She jumps up and down

Oh look at my dog
She is as small as a frog

When you see her run
Boy is it fun

To know she is happy
Makes me so glad

The thing I love about my dog is she's never bad.

Caroline Laird (8)
Bleary Primary School

Hallowe'en Night

It was a dark and stormy night
Everyone was shivering with fright
It was very very late
As we reached the graveyard gate
There he appeared
With his long white beard
Standing all alone
By the gravestone
He looked straight at me
As I fell to my knees he came over
And bent close to my ear
The words I shall always fear
Boo!

Sherrie Percy (8)
Bleary Primary School

The Swimmer

As he walks to his lane
The crowd cheers.
He is introduced over the microphone
And everyone's eyes look towards Lane Three
The middle lane and the fast lane.
The swimmer raises his arms
And waves to the crowd,
He removes his flip flops
And his tracksuit bottoms.
He takes off his T-shirt
And sets all his clothes
On a chair behind the timekeepers,
Standing only in his leggings,
Which cling to his frail legs,
He dons his red swim hat
And pulls it tightly over his ears.
After flexing again his little shoulders
And swivelling his arms like propellers
He secures his goggles
And mounts the blocks, crouches
Waiting on the hooter
To sound his release, his escape.
Now he is free, he is happy
That the wait is over.
As he thrusts and glides down the pool
Fifteen strokes and a tumble-turn
A push off the wall and home again.
The swimmer is the winner!

Philip Wilson (9)
Bleary Primary School

Spiderman

His name is Peter Parker
He's really rather shy
He lives in a New York apartment
He's just a normal guy.

On a field trip he did go
Along came a spider and bit him on the toe
From that day on things were never the same
Spiderman became his name.

Spiderman is so cool
Even though he looks like a fool
He thinks he is cool
Swinging on a kangaroo.

As a bad person you will fall
When Spiderman swings from wall to wall
You will be black and blue
When he gets through with you.

Tyler Houston (8)
Bleary Primary School

My Dog

I have a little dog,
And he jumps like a frog.
He is a little twit sometimes!
But I don't mind.
He sleeps in his house all night,
But in the morning it's quite a sight.
He comes inside for meals,
But sometimes from the cupboard little extras he steals
He's always chewing on his toy bone,
And when I'm at school he's all alone.
So anyone who wants a little friend,
A little puppy dog - I recommend!

Louise Megaw (8)
Bleary Primary School

Jack Frost

A little son and a wife he had
Being away at Christmas made him sad
One snowy night on his way home
He was driving along feeling alone.

Down came a storm
And the car lost control
With a skid to the right, it started to roll
Sam was no more, it became very cold.

Jack Frost comes prancing into the night
Dashing here and there out of sight,
Like the snow on the ground,
He was whiter than white.

To his house he did go,
Finding his son playing in the snow
Jack came home to say goodbye
With a hug and a kiss and a tear in his eye.

Jordan Houston (8)
Bleary Primary School

My Dog

My dog is really cool
She eats her lunch without a drool
She has a slipper for a toy and
She gives me such a lot of joy
Her coat is brown and black and
When she's on her lead she likes a lot of slack
She has a shiny black nose and
A long, long coat that always grows
She's playful and barks at us to play
She wants us to stay and play all day
She loves food and little treats
And when she behaves we give her snacks
And sometimes sweets.

Joanne Kelly (8)
Bleary Primary School

My Journey To Space

Three, two, one, up the rocket blasts,
Going up to space really really fast.
With flames from its tail and a pointy nose,
This rocket will take me where I want to go.

I think I'll go to Venus,
Or maybe stop at Mars.
I'll visit Pluto first of all,
Before I count the stars.

I wonder if there's life up here,
Will I have anything to fear.
Little men with bright green faces,
Taking me away and leaving no traces.

I think I'll just go to the moon,
I will ask the man if he's got any room.
For me to stop for a little while,
Tell him some jokes and make him smile.

Now it's time to say goodbye
Into my rocket and home I fly.
Back to Earth with a bump I go,
Just in time for school I know.

Joshua Cairns (8)
Bleary Primary School

Global Warming!

They say there's global warming,
Well I don't really know,
I opened the front door yesterday,
And I was covered in snow.
I'm sitting here all frozen,
I can't get out nor in,
It's minus one hundred,
And there's icicles on my chin.
They say there's global warming,
Well I would love to see,
Just out the window,
Instead I've forty blankets on my knee.
I phoned the air rescue,
They said they'll be here soon,
They'll put my dinner down the chimney
By Friday afternoon.
I switched on the TV
The snowploughs are moving fast,
Oh yes, oh yes, it's getting warmer,
Minus ninety-eight at last.
I feel like I'm trapped,
I'm in a snow covered hole,
I'm moving somewhere warmer,
I've bought an igloo in the North Pole!

Matthew Johnston (8)
Bleary Primary School

My Dog

My dog is so funny,
She acts like a bunny,
She plays with a frisbee,
And now it's all crispy.
She jumps too high off the ground,
Now there's a hole, you better beware.
She is a wee troublemaker,
And now my ice cream maker,
Has turned into a duster.
My dog stares in the long grass,
She waits for the right moment, and then she pounces,
And also she howls and howls and howls,
And sometimes she even growls and growls.
I haven't even told you her name,
Dakota it is, and I'm to blame,
She's a Siberian husky, and there's no doubt,
She poos all the time, I could do without.
I love to make her hair so shiny,
Get a big brush and brush for hours.
She sits with her head up so high,
Just staring at the blue, blue sky.
Dakota's just great at football skill,
She dribbles with the ball, without a pill,
She's better than Arsenal's Thierry Henry,
So she'll be going to play at Highbury!

Cameron Burke (8)
Bleary Primary School

My Dog

My dog is funny
I'm sure he's a bunny
Hop, hop, hopping all around
Digging holes in the ground,
He really does bark
But only at the dogs in the park.
I really look like a clown
When I take him for a walk in the town,
He hasn't got matted fur
He's got black and white hair,
I think it's hard for him to jump
'Cause he's such a fat lump.
He only has half a tail
But we got him cheap in a sale,
Why can't he think he's a bear
Then at least maybe he'd scare.
I really can't stand the hound
But I'll miss him when he is in the ground!
My mum she treats pets like babies
I know that mad dog has rabies,
The cars he will chase
He think he's in a race.
Me thinks he's at top speed
But you want to see him wolfing his feed!

Shane Fleming (10)
Bleary Primary School

Friends

My best friend is leaving school,
She is so cool and,
Makes everyone drool,
She's got her own swimming pool.

But I don't want her to leave,
But it would have been bad if she,
Had left on Christmas Eve,
Why oh why does she have to leave.

We will all miss her,
It just really isn't fair,
And the rest of my friendship,
Will be all bare.

She's leaving in a day
I hope she'll visit us in May,
She is so sad,
And also is mad.

She's going in a few hours now,
Soon she'll be away,
Lying in the biggest bay,
With nothing to say.

She's going going and she's gone,
To get her back I would mow the lawn,
But it's too bad,
She's gone,
And she's never coming
Back.

Lauren Smith (9)
Bleary Primary School

Max

My dog Max loves to jump,
But sometimes knocks you down with a bump.
His tongue is pink, his nose is black,
With soft fur all down his back.

Max is a guard dog, I love to see,
He always jumps up on my knee.
The vet's table he does not like,
It always gives him a bit of a fright.

When we go for walks round the park,
Max will run, jump and bark.
He loves his food and bone and ball,
But he loves *me most of all!*

Chloe McKinley (8)
Bleary Primary School

Untidy Room

Smelly socks - a lot of frocks
Single bed - and teddy Ted
Little Joey on his head
Making no sound on the bed
Lots of clothes everywhere
Now the cupboard's really bare
It's as if my sister lives there
Because all these things belong to her!

Nicole McQuillan
Clea Primary School

The Room

A piece of hair
A gummy bear
Red comb,
Chicken bone,
On the floor is a ball,
With posters on the wall,
Big shocks
Of dirty socks
Underwear
Is everywhere
This is my brother's room!

Alyshea Smith (10)
Clea Primary School

My House

My Armagh room,
Mum's cleaning vacuum
The DVD
Followed by the TV
The arguing all night,
Becomes a big fight.
Mum's smelly broom
And the good living room.

Dáire Carr
Clea Primary School

The Sun

I can be so beautiful and so warm,
I can see my reflection when I look on
The roof of the barn.

I shine right down and turn people brown,
I brighten their day especially in May,
For the flowers they are in full bloom.

When I come down and brighten the day,
The big grey cloud goes far away.

When I come down every day and
Then go up
The only thing that barks at me is
The little farmyard pup.

Then at the end of the tiring day
I go far away
And wait for another big bright day.

Louise Hanna (11)
Donacloney Primary School

Storm

I can be so mad
Screaming around houses,
Thumping windows wildly and flinging papers all around,
I can rip off branches and
Throw acorns to the ground
Sometimes I kick dustbins
On purpose,
When I am hassled
I rave and roar from rooftops and
Alleyways.

Angus Orr (10)
Donacloney Primary School

Lightning

I can give people a terrible fright,
For in the dark sky I can make it all bright.

Children start crying when I show my face,
Flashes of colour all over the
Place.

I can set fire to trees and to
Flowers,
And scientists marvel at my special
Powers!

I am so scary I think you will agree,
I am the greatest,
I'm lightning you see.

Hannah Graham (11)
Donacloney Primary School

Football

F abulous fun
O ut of this world
O n the ball
T op game
B est sport
A ll the enjoyment you need
L ike sports
L ove *football.*

George Wilson (11)
Donacloney Primary School

Dear Betty . . .

Dear Betty
I am a window
Every downpour get soaked wet and dirty
No one bothers to clean me
Can I get no privacy?
Everyone looks straight through me,
Birds fly into me
It's like I'm invisible
The small people are the worst
Hitting me with dirty sticky hands
What should I do
To make them leave me alone?
Yours annoyingly
See through.

Becky Troughton (11)
Donacloney Primary School

Eleven Plus

E very child has a chance
L onging to do well
E arnestly they work
V aliant are those who try
E asy, who said it was
N ervewrecking to the end.

P arents are worse than children
L ogical most of the time
U neasy, when results are due
S uper, it's all over.

Bradley Martin (11)
Donacloney Primary School

My Family

M y family is brilliant
Y eah they are brilliant

F riends know my family
A nd my family know them
M y brother is annoying sometimes
 I sometimes feel like killing him
L ike in an annoying way
Y eah my family is great.

Carla Alderdice (9)
Donacloney Primary School

Hobbies

H is for horse riding
O is for obstacle
B is for basketball
B is for baseball as well
 I is for ice hockey
E is for enjoying
S is for swimming.

Ashleigh Meredith (9)
Donacloney Primary School

Horse

H orses are fast
O n a horse
R eady to go riding!
S table is clean
E ating apples!

Emma Sinnamon (10)
Donacloney Primary School

What About Me!

Once I went to my friend's birthday,
I felt a little bit shy,
I really, really hated the ice cream
But loved the blueberry pie.

I ate a little too much you know,
OK, maybe a lot.
Then it was present time,
I got her a cot.

She was getting all the attention,
But no, not me.
You see me and her don't get on
But her mum invited me.

She was boasting a lot,
Which started to annoy me,
But then it slipped out,
What about me?

Natasha Murphy (10)
Donacloney Primary School

Sandy

Sandy is my puppy
She lives in her shed
Where she has a nice warm bed

She's a greedy little puppy
She gobbles down her food
But she's very friendly and quite good.

She plays in my garden
Football's her favourite game
That is why I like her
Because my sport's the same.

Mark Neill (10)
Donacloney Primary School

Winter Days

W inter days are full of snow,
 I watch, but I see nothing grow
N obody can I see
T hough look, it's Frostie and me
E veryone came out to play
R obin jumps down and starts to say

D ay is breaking
A h! Go away little robin and stop craking
Y ou see a single snowflake, as it falls
S oon everyone is throwing snowballs.

Rebekah Alexander (9)
Donacloney Primary School

Rangers

R angers are my favourite team
A ren't they just the best?
N obody can beat them
G o on try your best
E very time they play a game
R anger's fans go wild
S o don't be sad, cos I am glad that I'm a
    Ranger's child!

Cathy Orr (9)
Donacloney Primary School

Family

F amilies like mine are great
A lways having fun
M y brothers are full of mischief, always on the run
 I have an older sister
L iving with her is such a pain
Y ou would think she was my mum!

Lynn Savage (9)
Donacloney Primary School

Football

F ootball crazy
O ver the bar
O n the pitch
T ackles the goalie
B all goes out
A fter the first half
L ong time left to go
L et's go and play another game.

Matthew Davidson (10)
Donacloney Primary School

Flowers

F lowers smell nice
L et there be light
O pen the petals
W ater to grow
E ager to rise
R ain falls on them
S weet smelling scent can be smelt for miles.

Lauren Nicholson (10)
Donacloney Primary School

Lorry

L orries big and small
O ver the roads they go
R iding along delivering to all
R oaring through all weathers, rain, sleet or snow
Y ou see them passing by each day.

Andrew Totten (10)
Donacloney Primary School

Ideas

Ideas can pop up in our heads at night,
Even before it is light.
Ideas can show up at any time,
When we're busy working from nine to five.
Or when eating and drinking or just playing about.

I wish I had an idea about poems.
Something that rhymes so I could show them.
So next time you get an idea that's good,
Quick! Grab a notebook and don't be a fool!

Zoe Beckett (10)
Donacloney Primary School

Rangers FC

R angers are the best
A nd Rangers score and the score is now 3-0
N o! they've hacked Michael Mols
G oal!
E ven if Rangers lose we will still follow on
R ound up the fans, we need a picture
S cotland, Rangers for ever.

F ootball crazy, Rangers mad!
C ome on Rangers!

Simon Hodgett (9)
Donacloney Primary School

Flood

F loods spread over land
L ike a leak from an ocean
O ver and up they are there
O ut fast, not in slow motion
D angerous floods.

David Sinnamon (8)
Donacloney Primary School

Moonlight

M agical, moonlight, mentality cool
O bvious amazing outstanding and new
O verflowing with stars nice and bright
N early like starlight, bright as well
L ovely and light, just as I like
I mpossible to take it away
G ood and giant, big and grey
H alf of whole, happy and high
T he light makes me twinkle all night!

John Moore (9)
Donacloney Primary School

Football

F ootball is the best sport
O ne day I want to play for Linfield
O n Saturday I will practise
T he centre-half clears
B irmingham City get beaten by Man Utd
A nd the crowd goes wild with excitement
L infield beat Glentoran, *Yes!*
L ate for practice!

Andrew Daly (10)
Donacloney Primary School

Tornado

T ornado: big, black and scary
O rdinary wind gets stronger, bigger
R ough as a hedgehog!
N othing he can't pick up
A bandon the city before you or get
    scooped up by its whirlpool
D o it before you fly into the sky!
O utstanding wind finally comes to an end.

Jason Lamont (8)
Donacloney Primary School

Pretty Petals

P retty flowers in your garden
R eally catch your eye
E very time they blossom
T hey give you pretty petals!
T heir scent is most charming
Y ou'll love them for ever.

P etals can be any colour
E ven when they're picked
T o put into a shiny glass vase
A lways will make you smile
L ovely shapes and patterns
S eem to smile at you when you smile at them!

Hannah Whittaker (8)
Donacloney Primary School

Moonlight

M oonlight, light and bright
O ver the moon, it's really shiny
O h the moon white and light
N ever dark
L ight, is colourful and beautiful
I see how bright it is on Hallowe'en night
G round lights up like the moon on a winter night
H igh up in the sky
T he moon is light and white.

Jordan Gibson (8)
Donacloney Primary School

Thunder

T hunder crackles in the moonlight
H igh in the sky
U nderneath the clouds
N eed to turn your electricity off
D angerous in the sky
E nergy
R ain falls as well.

Nicole Mount (9)
Donacloney Primary School

Rainbow

R ain
A gainst sun
I nteresting colours
N atural
B eautiful
O range rays
W onderful.

Sophie Fleming (9)
Donacloney Primary School

Tiger

T iger, tiger in the zoo
I ntelligent indeed
G oing to kill anything in its way
E ager to attack its prey
R eady to pounce on you!

James Hall (9)
Donacloney Primary School

Friends

A good friend is someone

Who cares about you
Who plays with you
Who never leaves you
Who is trustworthy
Who is kind to you
Who gives you good advice
Who you can rely on
Who doesn't get you into trouble
Who helps you with your work
Who helps you tidy up
Who cheers you up
Who doesn't bully you
Who is generous
Who is not jealous
Who is helpful
Who gives you birthday presents

A good friend is priceless!

Hayley Johnston (9)
Edenderry Primary School

In Winter I Like . . .

Still snow as more falls around it
Happy faces as we warm up the fire
When it is lit
I sit drinking a cup of hot chocolate
Everyone slipping and sliding on ice
Sunsets very early at night
Bare trees standing up straight
Closing the gate
As the frost falls off.

Megan Robinson (8)
Edenderry Primary School

In Winter I Like . . .

The fire blazing in the living room
The fog spreading across the country
Building a snowman
Dark nights

Frozen ponds
Red holly berries
Trees that are bare
Snow falling down.

Jordan Deering (8)
Edenderry Primary School

In Winter I Like . . .

The foggy mist in the morning
The icy world around you
The bare trees
Making snowmen and putting hats on them
Going for a walk just in time for the sunset
Seeing the prickly holly leaves on the holly trees.

Hannah Lyttle (7)
Edenderry Primary School

Winter

Soft snow falling
Mighty wind blowing
Poor robin searching
Green holly growing
Jolly snowman melting
Black clouds disappearing.

Lucy Daly (7)
Edenderry Primary School

Leaves

Leaves brown, leaves crunchy,
Leaves yellow, leaves crinkly,
Leaves orange, leaves tiny,
Leaves gold, leaves shiny,
Leaves falling gently.

Leaves big, leaves small,
Leaves short, leaves tall,
Leaves fat, leaves thin,
Leaves that go in the bin.

Patrick Ortega (7)
Edenderry Primary School

Winter

Enormous snowmen shivering,
Naked branches swaying,
Frozen snowballs falling,
Jagged icicles dripping,
Cheerful robins cheeping,
Slushy ice melting.

Rebecca Roberts (8)
Edenderry Primary School

Peace

Peace is relaxing in the sun
Peace is a warm breeze
Peace is the sound of the waves splashing
Peace is the birds singing
Peace is when you doze off
But No Fighting.

Victoria Argue (10)
Edenderry Primary School

Peace

Peace is birds singing
And the leaves rustling on the trees
Peace is the sun shining
And a nice gentle breeze
But peace is not children shouting out loud
Peace is lying in bed
With the cat purring in the background
Peace is not working all day long.

Alexander Hawthorne (9)
Edenderry Primary School

Peace

Peace is when the birds are singing
Peace is when you are lying dozing
Peace is when the streams are flowing
Peace is when there is a warm breeze blowing
Peace is when lawnmowers are humming
But real peace is when there is no fighting.

Andrew Steele (10)
Edenderry Primary School

Peace

Relaxing
Watching TV
Talking in background
Lying in my bed
Kindness.

Jade Megaw (9)
Edenderry Primary School

Peace

Peace is
Sunbathing
Warm breeze
Birds singing
Trees swaying
Waves crashing on the rocks
Peace is no fighting
Smell of the flowers
People cutting grass
Sleeping in a comfortable bed
But the real peace is to be
Kind to everyone.

Kirsty Burns (9)
Edenderry Primary School

Peace

No fighting,
Smell of the flowers,
Floating in the water on my back,
Children playing,
Dozing in bed,
On a Saturday morning.

Darren Leckey (10)
Edenderry Primary School

The Melody Of Love

A melody is a tune of love
That only one can hear.
For the heart sings like a dove,
For only you, my dear.

I see all the love that's in your heart,
And hope that you will too.
For if that melody should start,
I will eternally love you.

For this melody my love,
Is very hard to kill.
I shall love you for evermore
Even if you do not love me I know I will.

This heart of mine is your song,
So use it as you wish.
I love you and always will,
Collect my love, if you want, in a pink
And rosemary dish.

Listen please my love
I want you to know
I will always love you
I've been trying to show
For the human spirit doesn't last that long
But the melody of my love can make
You a whole song.

Robyn-Dee Herdman (10)
Maghaberry Primary School

You

Flowers are pretty like your face
Roses are red like your heart
Chocolates are sweet like your lips
Violets are blue like your eyes
I will let you lead the way
And I will pay for you
And every time I see roses
I will think of you.

Colin Tinsley (10)
Maghaberry Primary School

Quickly

Quickly the horse trotted up the hill
Quickly the man leapt into his car
Quickly the fans charged out of Croke Park
Quickly the snow built up on the Earth
Quickly the whale ducked under the water
Quickly the lion ran to the lioness.

Carrie Mallon (11)
St John's Primary School, Middletown

Noisily

Noisily the great big dog howled in the misty night
Noisily the aeroplane landed in the enormous airport
Noisily the big black bull roared for his food
Noisily the rain clashed on the roof
Noisily the dictionary smacked down on the table
Noisily the volcano erupted.

Paschal Carvill (11)
St John's Primary School, Middletown

Time

I had some fun
At one.

I saw my friend
At two.

I broke my knee
At three.

I went to court
At four.

I saw a hive
At five.

I ate a Twix
At six.

I saw Heaven
At seven.

I saw a saint
At eight.

I went to dine
At nine.

I saw Ben
At ten.

Plunkett Hart (11)
St John's Primary School, Middletown

Quietly

Quietly the man sneaked swiftly into the house
Quietly the wind howled in the trees
Quietly the wolf crept through the forest to catch the deer
Quietly the dog howled at the stranger
Quietly the rain smacked the ground
Quietly the swan moved through the water.

Barry Trainor (10)
St John's Primary School, Middletown

A Strange Poem

I saw a fish eating a dish
I saw a table play in a stable

I saw a pie wear a tie
I saw a mat bite a rat

I saw a dog eat a frog
I saw a log run and jog

I saw a boat jump on a goat
I saw a ball shop in a mall

I saw a hare on the mare
I saw a balloon sit on the moon

I saw a pin fight with the bin
I saw a CD eat a TV

I saw a box eat a fox

I finally leave the strange town
While the sun goes down.

Karen McCann (10)
St John's Primary School, Middletown

Adverb Poem

Quickly the eagle shot across the sky
Quietly the snake was hunting its prey
Heavily the elephant stomped to its home
Coldly the boys fingers froze in the snow
Noisily the lion roared in pain
Brightly the sun has stopped the rain
Sleepily I had to get out of bed
Slowly the turtle went on ahead.

Keith Moran (11)
St John's Primary School, Middletown

A Very Strange Poem

I saw a box
eat a fox

I saw a ship
eat a chip

I saw Harry Potter
eat a locker

I saw my mate
eat a gate

I saw a hen
by a pen

I saw a pencil
change into a stencil

I saw a bomb
sing a song

Do you believe me?
I swear it's true
because there's only one
girl who believes me too.

Shauna Mooney (10)
St John's Primary School, Middletown

Silently

Silently the day slipped to night
Silently the baby hushed to sleep
Silently the blackthorn turned to white
Silently the lake sparkled to ice
Silently the grass was covered with snow
Silently the rain faded away
Silently the story came to an end.

Kerri McQuaid (10)
St John's Primary School, Middletown

A Strange Story

I saw a fish climb a tree
I saw a lamp eat a bumblebee

I saw some grass go to school
I saw a wall swim in a pool

I saw a cloud on the ground
I saw a square look so round

I saw the sun inside the moon
I saw a table dance with a baboon

I saw a book eat a bin
I saw a TV say his sins

What I saw is really true
So come along and see it too.

Orlagh Curry (11)
St John's Primary School, Middletown

A Strange Poem

I saw a fox making a box
I saw a tree making some tea
I saw a man drive a pan
I saw a fish eating a dish
I saw a pen eating a crayon
I saw a clock eating a bat
I saw a balloon sit on the moon
I saw an otter eating Harry Potter

Do you believe that I'm telling the truth
Because if you do . . .

Louise McGuigan (10)
St John's Primary School, Middletown

Strange Poem

I saw a door
dance on the floor

I saw a pen
attack a hen

I saw a clock
play with a frock

I saw a rat
eating a cat

I saw a log
sit on a dog

I saw a pie
eating a fly

I saw an egg
fight a peg

I saw a pool
go to school

And now I leave this strange town
As the sun comes floating down.

Aoife O'Hagan (11)
St John's Primary School, Middletown

Noisily

Noisily the cheetah scampered away into the water
Noisily the mouse scattered into his home
Noisily the boy crept in the long grass
Noisily the class chatted away in the hall
Noisily my feet wobbled in the field
Noisily the leaves swept along the path.

Catherine Spottiswood (10)
St John's Primary School, Middletown

A Strange Story

I saw a bun holding a gun
I saw a chair eat a bear

I saw a sheep chase Little Bo Peep
I saw a rock hold a lock

I saw a poster beat a toaster
I saw a pen punch a hen

I saw a plaster teach a master

All that I told you is really true and
This one girl believes me too.

Jade Hegarty (10)
St John's Primary School, Middletown

Happily!

Happily the sun greets the morning sky
Happily the flowers watch the clouds go by
Happily the animals scampered down to the stream
To cool themselves down from the warm sun beams.

Happily the grass stares up at the trees
Happily the flowers watch the busy bees
Happily the moon chats to Mars
While all around appear the twinkling stars.

Andrea Shine (11)
St John's Primary School, Middletown

Strange Poem

I saw a pie as a magpie
I saw a sheep driving a jeep
I saw a minx it was pink
I saw a house eat a mouse
I saw a snake run away
I saw the sun it was like a bun
I saw a balloon sleep in a cocoon
I saw Big Ben on top of two men
Ten men saw it at ten too.

Philip Sherry (11)
St John's Primary School, Middletown

Strange Poem

I saw a map doing a rap
I saw a tree watch TV
I saw money eating honey
I saw some art driving a cart
I saw jewels steal from pools
I saw a bus turn a corner
I saw a tractor turn into a field
I saw some babies they had a car
I saw a turtle go 1000 mph
I saw some sand play in a band
I saw a chair it was growing hair.

Cathal Harnett (11)
St John's Primary School, Middletown

Under My Bed

Under my bed is a book and a sock
and an old frock, a sweet wrapper too
and bowl full of stew.

Under my bed is for me.

Under my bed is magical with shooting stars
that fill the sky, and a piece of blueberry pie

Under my bed belongs to me.

Under my bed is a dressed up witch,
and a multicoloured fish.

Under my bed is a secret
Under my bed is mine.

Sinead Gillen (10)
St Malachy's Primary School, Armagh

Armagh

Gloves catch
Boots clash
Spot kick
Crowds arise
Whistle blows
McGeeney scores
Sam coming
Joe jumping
Ref rushing
Sub on
Photographers clicking
Match programmes flicking
Just feel the footballs song!

John Maguire (9)
St Malachy's Primary School, Armagh

My Sister

My sister is a . . .
hardworking and never gives up
. . . kind of sister.

She is a . . .
take you to the movies and
buy you popcorn
. . . kind of sister.

She is a . . .
watch the soaps, raid the cupboards
and blame it on you!
. . . kind of sister.

She is a . . .
go outside and play,
just get out of my way,
change the channel
that's boring
. . . kind of sister.

She is a . . .
go to bed and don't
annoy my head,
football and sports are so boring
. . . kind of sister.

And this lovely sister is mine, all mine.

Fionnuala McKenna (10)
St Malachy's Primary School, Armagh

My Gran

My gran is a . . .
watch TV sitting in a chair
. . . kind of gran.

She is a . . .
go put something warm on you
funny sort of gran who makes you laugh
. . . kind of gran.

She is a . . .
hot water bottle for your sore tummy
do you want a packet of crisps?
do your homework before you go out
. . . kind of gran.

She is a . . .
be good at school
shh don't tell nobody
go up to the graveyard in the car
go to bed early
. . . kind of gran.

She is a . . .
give you more sweets than anyone else
it's a lovely day go out and play
come on in, you look cold
did you have your dinner yet?
. . . kind of gran

And this lovely gran is mine, all mine.

Nola Boylan (9)
St Malachy's Primary School, Armagh

My Dad

My dad is a . . .
sit down and watch the football
. . . kind of dad.

He is a . . .
shout at the TV like me
I'm hungry, I need dinner
. . . kind of dad.

He is a . . .
blast up the music
I never get sick
I'm as solid as a brick
. . . kind of dad.

He is a . . .
computer whizz
maths genius
I'm going for the papers
I'm away for a pint
. . . kind of dad.

He is a . . .
finish your dinner
go get my slippers
tell me a joke
what's the craic
. . . kind of dad

And this cool dad is mine, all mine!

Luke Grimley (9)
St Malachy's Primary School, Armagh

My Mum

My mum is a . . .
worry a lot about her hair
. . . kind of mum.

She is a . . .
put your tie on keep it neat
don't have smelly feet
. . . kind of mum.

She is a . . .
make you better with a cuddle
what you need's a cup of chocolate
take your time
. . . kind of mum.

She is a . . .
comfort, cuddle, caring
grateful, surprising
let's make coffee
sit by the fire
. . . kind of mum.

She is a . . .
video watching
popcorn eating
tidy your bed
want sweets
. . . kind of mum.

And this lovely mum is mine, all mine.

Karen Traynor (10)
St Malachy's Primary School, Armagh

Under My Bed

Under my bed is snow
A smelly old sock
And a lollipop
The smell of a beach
A forgotten ice cream maker
Under my bed is for me.

Under my bed is a body
A hairy old spider
And a party popper
My P4 homework book
The skin of a pear
Under my bed belongs to me.

Under my bed is a bear
And a very old clip
And a zip
Under my bed is a secret.

Under my bed is a doll
And a burst ball
A telephone call
That is what is under my bed.

Carreann Nugent (9)
St Malachy's Primary School, Armagh

My Gran

My gran is a . . .
give you lots of sweets
. . . kind of gran.

She is a . . .
have lots of fun
buy you a bun
. . . kind of gran.

She is a . . .
you don't have to eat your dinner
don't worry you'll always be a winner
does this dress make me look thinner?
. . . kind of gran.

She is a . . .
put on your coat and don't get a cold
listen to your mother and don't be bold,
you are getting very old
do what you are told
. . . kind of gran.

And this lovely grandmother is mine all mine!

Tiernan Leonard (9)
St Malachy's Primary School, Armagh

Under My Bed

Under my bed is last week's newspaper.
The blood from a horse and a cow
that is grazing
The sock of my brother.
Under my bed is for me.

Under my bed there are rats droppings.
A dehydrated dung beetle and some 100 year old dust.
There is a dirty nappy.
Under my bed belongs to me.

Under my bed is Bloody Sunday and
times tables that can never be answered.
There is a pile of dino dung under my bed
Under my bed is secret.

Under my bed there are snots from a rat.
The Guinness Book of Records 3000
and the lid of a glue.
Under my bed is mine.

Under my bed are pictures of Mars.
The wrapper of a Wonka bar.

This is what is under my bed.

Stephen King (10)
St Malachy's Primary School, Armagh

My Gran

My gran is a . . .
Mrs Bucket double lookalike
. . . kind of gran.

She is a . . .
'one little sweet won't hurt'
sew a few stitches on your skirt
. . . kind of gran.

She is a . . .
go to Mass every day,
kind and loving
tell you a story
. . . kind of gran.

She is a . . .
laugh at your jokes,
bake you a scone,
give you a hug when you're sad,
'don't worry it can be cleaned up,'
. . . kind of gran.

She is a . . .
'don't cry,'
'you can tell a tiny lie,'
get you whatever you want
warm and cosy
. . . kind of gran.

And this lovely grandmother is mine all mine!

Bronagh Grimley (10)
St Malachy's Primary School, Armagh

My Auntie

My auntie is a . . .
trip to the park
. . . kind of auntie.

She is a . . .
extra little sweet won't hurt
come on with me
. . . kind of auntie.

She is a . . .
do you want this?
did you miss me?
I love you
. . . kind of auntie.

She is a . . .
I'll be your best friend
you're going to be fine
is my make-up alright?
do you like this?
. . . kind of auntie.

She is a . . .
how have you been?
who have you seen?
do you like your red coat?
here's a sweet for your sore throat
. . . kind of auntie.

And this lovely auntie
Is mine all mine.

Zoe McGirr (10)
St Malachy's Primary School, Armagh

Under My Bed

Under my bed is a boring old bag,
And a hairy old spider.
An African mask
A tatty old doll
And a blue winter scarf.
There is a magical world under my bed,
And an African Safari.
Under my bed is for me.

Under my bed is a dancing warlock,
And a flying Maths sheet.
A wicked old witch granting a wish
But in the wrong sort of way.
Under my bed belongs to me.

Under my bed is the Eiffel Tower
An ocean of blood with a fish
There is also mice having a picnic
Under my bed is a secret.

Under my bed is a million pound bill.
A smothered school
Under my bed is mine
So hands off!

Rebecca O'Reilly (10)
St Malachy's Primary School, Armagh

My Auntie

My auntie is a . . .
playing games lots of fun
. . . kind of auntie.

She is a . . .
driving cars and go on a journey
I'll be OK don't you worry
. . . kind of auntie.

She is a . . .
take you to the shop
and buy you a lollipop
. . . kind of auntie.

She is a . . .
come on in and make a milkshake
or a big juicy cream cake
come on down to the lake now
what else could we make?
. . . kind of auntie.

And that lovely auntie is mine all mine!

April Flynn (9)
St Malachy's Primary School, Armagh

Earth

People dying
Bombs flying
Sea pollution
Children fighting
People hunting
Animals dying
People smoking
Children scream
Just listen
To the
Earth's song.

Connor Traynor (9)
St Malachy's Primary School, Armagh

What Is Green?

Green is the colour of grass
And a tree
And a little green pea.
It's healthy and smart
And very tidy and neat.
It's a leaf and
The quietness of silent stars.
Vitamins and broccoli
Both are green.
Troublesome tables
And green labels.
So are some winter hats
And baldy-cats.
Turtles are green
And a healthy bean.
The happy look of fun
And a poisoned bun.
Pus is green
And always seen.
Tights, kites
And green lights.
Leprechaun top
And hip hop.
A deadly disease
And a blown-out sneeze.
Envy is green
And ivy too.
They wear green soft gloves
When they are pinching you.

Deirdre O'Reilly (10)
St Malachy's Primary School, Armagh

Earth

Trees cut
Trees born
Animals killed
Streets dirty
People smoke
Children bereaved
People die
Bombs fly
Blood spilt
People cry
Dust flies
Birds fly
Gun shots
Children run
Just listen
To the
Earth's song.

Martyn Kenny (9)
St Malachy's Primary School, Armagh

Earth

Trees burn
Children crying
Wars starting
People dying
Hunters come
Guns shout
Animals run
Adults smoke
Children breathe
Everyone cheers
Just feel
Earth song.

Tara Kelly (9)
St Malachy's Primary School, Armagh

Niamh

Loves dolls,
Always falls,
Gets ice cream,
When she screams.
Wants to be a rock star,
And play a guitar
Copycat,
But I don't mind that
Loses things,
Like my rings.
She'll do things,
You'll never believe,
That's my little sister
Her name's Niamh.

Larisa Gribben (11)
St Patrick's Primary School, Armagh

Caoili

Little clown
Walks around
Very funny
Gives me money
Hates rain
It makes her insane
A superstar
Loves chocolate bars
Loves chips
With no dips
Quad crazy
Not lazy
Comical really
That's our Caoili.

Aaron Hannon (10)
St Patrick's Primary School, Armagh

Deborah

Make-up girl
Has a pearl
Shiny eyes
Loves fries
Gives me money
Calls me honey
Loves hair
Does stare
Likes to eat
Hates meat
Can cook
Bit of a spook
Not from France
But she can dance
Loves Gareth Gates
And washing plates.

Michael McCartney (10)
St Patrick's Primary School, Armagh

My Brother

X Box fan
He thinks he's the man
Always hits me
His trousers fit me
Listens to rock
Hair sticks up a lot
Wears baggy jeans
Loves baked beans
Hangs with Liam
Who's very plain.

Ruairi O'Kane (10)
St Patrick's Primary School, Armagh

My Sister Tracy

Animal lover,
Make-up taker.
Clean girl,
Shines her room.
Big time dreams,
It would seem.
Time to eat,
She hates meat.
Takes a smoke,
Die of a stroke.
Likes to rap,
Hates reading maps.
She thinks she's cute,
But eats too much fruit.

Rory Howard (11)
St Patrick's Primary School, Armagh

My Sister Denise

Good singer
Hard puncher
Beautiful hair
Dirty stare
Football lover
Speedy runner
Art fantastic
Her cooking is drastic
Fussy eater
Chess cheater.

Naomi Campbell (11)
St Patrick's Primary School, Armagh

Winter Wonderland

The snow tumbled down from the grey sky,
It lies like a white carpet on the icy ground.
The snowflakes glitter in the morning sun.
The thin ice hangs from the trees like wind chimes.
I put on my hat, scarf, gloves, tights and my warm coat.
I ran outside to put on my ice skating boots and the poor
lonely kitten stood freezing on the ice.

Dearbhla Murphy (10)
St Patrick's Primary School, Armagh

Wintertime

The tiny robin stands freezing on my window sill.
It is looking for some bread and nuts.
When I look out of my window,
I see some tiny prints of the robin.
I put on my welly boots.
It is cold outside but I go to feed
the little robin.

Shane Mallon (11)
St Patrick's Primary School, Armagh

Winter Wonderland

Winter is here.
Trees are bare.
I try to catch a white snowflake.
I feed the birds nuts and seeds.

Lisa Crossen (9)
St Patrick's Primary School, Armagh

Winter Wonderland

The trees are losing their leaves.
Feel the cold breeze hitting your face.
The animals curl up to keep themselves
warm.
The children play happily in the snow,
Their face, their nose, their fingers glow.
Night time comes and all is white,
The silver moon makes everything bright.

Nathan Young (10)
St Patrick's Primary School, Armagh

Winter Wonderland

The snow tumbles down from the sky.
The ground is hard that the birds can't get food.
The tree has lost all of its leaves.
It stands cold and bare.
Winter is here everything is frozen.
The snowflakes crunch beneath my shoes.
My fingers and toes are numb.

Cailin Kennedy (10)
St Patrick's Primary School, Armagh

Winter Is Here

The snow falls quickly from the sky
It's already here you can't deny
The snow comes down from the sky above
Tumbling like a snowflake does
The robin is hungry, so hungry, and is
Searching for food.
The hedgehog is hibernating in the wood.

Shay McGahan (11)
St Patrick's Primary School, Armagh

My Three Fish

My fish swim
They are very slim

They are called Orange, Silver and Gold
I hope they'll grow old.

I like their fins
They look like little pins.

When one of them died
I cried and cried.

Lauren Guy (8)
St Patrick's Primary School, Armagh

Duty

Monday in the playground
Tuesday in our class
Wednesday marking homework
Thursday playing on the grass
Friday going to library
Saturday put my feet up
Sunday going to Mass
Monday starts again.

Rebecca McGeary (9)
St Patrick's Primary School, Armagh

Teacher

T is for teaching
E is for education
A is for awards
C is for checking work
H is for hearing reading
E is for English poems
R is for rhyming words.

Aidan Campbell (9)
St Patrick's Primary School, Armagh

Every Day

Bears growl
Wolves howl
Lions roar
Larks soar
Eagles glide
Cats hide
Kangaroos jump
Caterpillars hump
Tigers stalk
People walk
Horses clop
Rabbits hop
Snails are slow
Night flies glow.

Kevin McAleavey (8)
St Patrick's Primary School, Armagh

Jump Or Jiggle

Bears growl
Wolves howl
Snakes slide
Seagulls glide
Dogs bark
While in the park
Lions roar
Pigs snore
Frogs jump
Caterpillars hump
Horses clop
Rabbits hop.

Natalie Malone (9)
St Patrick's Primary School, Armagh

Animals

Bears growl
Wolves howl
Cats pounce
Dogs bounce
Rabbits hop
Horses clop
Skunks stink
That's what I think!

Kevin Aherne (8)
St Patrick's Primary School, Armagh

Animals

Bears growl just like my dad
Wolves howl very very bad
Pigs grunt just too loud
Predators don't go with the crowd
Grasshoppers leap
Cows munch to eat
Birds glide
Mice just hide
But I'm normal!

Jack Hughes (9)
St Patrick's Primary School, Armagh

Animals

Bears growl
Wolves howl
Kangaroos kick
Kittens lick
Pigs are pink
Skunks stink
Cheetahs are fast
Tortoise comes last.

Mark Murphy (8)
St Patrick's Primary School, Armagh

Animals

Lions roar
Hedgehogs snore
Dogs bark
In the dark
Birds nest
Chickens rest
Wolves hunt
Pigs grunt
Snake slide
Eagles glide
Foxes hide
And horses
We ride.

Sean Perry (9)
St Patrick's Primary School, Armagh

Arctic

Snow wolves howl
and prowl.
Polar bears eat
to produce heat.
Fish swooping
and swirling
While deer prance
and dance.
Penguins waddle
and say
'Living in the cold
is a doddle.'

Johnny Bergin (8)
St Patrick's Primary School, Armagh

My Dog Misty

I love my dog because she's so cute,
She's a real hoot.

She's eleven weeks old
And sometimes she's bold.

I got her in the pound,
In the lost and found.

She barks at the cat
Mummy says, 'Don't do that!'

She's a collie cross
She likes to be boss!

She's black and white,
And yelps all night.

She loves going outside
She always looks for somewhere to hide.

She's not toilet trained yet,
But soon will be I bet!

Hollie Johnston (9)
St Patrick's Primary School, Armagh

Animals

Lions roar
Larks soar

Hens flap
Crocodiles snap

Kangaroos bounce
While tigers pounce

Whales dive
But me and my dad we
Just *drive.*

Cailin McGeown (9)
St Patrick's Primary School, Armagh

Back To School

When I went back to school
Everyone was so quick
Because I was off sick.
Everyone knew how to do this
Everyone knew how to do that
While I was left wondering what?
Hollie had bought a new coat
Natalie had bought a new boat
Rebecca had bought a new rat
Lauren had bought a new hat
Caron had made a new friend
And Emma was round the bend.
After a day all I could say
Everything was back to OK!

Edel Donnelly (9)
St Patrick's Primary School, Armagh

Spell Rap

Trouble and strife
Get a life
Hubble and bubble
Always in trouble
Hocus pocus
Holy smokus.

Bat's eyes bad breath
Now what's left!
Smelly shoes
Oh and smelly socks
All mixed together
For a spell that rocks.

Sean O'Neill (8)
St Patrick's Primary School, Armagh

Colours And Senses

Black is for the moonlit sky.
Yellow is for the sun in the morning sunrise.
Red is the fence in my garden.
Orange and white are for the Armagh flag.

I love the smell of the cool, cool breeze.
I love the smell of the steam coming out of the kettle.
I hate the feeling of a dark red rose; it prickles and tickles on
my little, little nose.
I really, really like the feeling of the spring onion chips in my mouth.

Aisling White (7)
St Patrick's Primary School, Armagh

My Horse Sparkles

She gallops and canters all around
Her tail swishing and swaying from side to side
Begging me to saddle up and ride.

When I'm riding on Sparkles back
She trots while I guide her down the track
She whines and neighs and shakes her head
It must be time for her to be fed.

Lauren Mackle (8)
St Patrick's Primary School, Armagh

Farmyard

Cows have calves
Pigs have piglets
Hens have chicks
And they are small
Horses have foals
And they are tall.

Matthew Rice (9)
St Patrick's Primary School, Armagh

Skateboarding

Skateboarding, skateboarding
Oh, what great fun!
Watch my stylish tricks everyone
Japan, Kick Flip
And Superman too
They all must seem impossible to you.

My friends skate with me, we laugh and have fun
As we race past each other
One by one
Down steep slopes
And up the next one.

Exhilarating races man what a thrill
But safety equipment's a must
In case there's a *spill*.
Always have a helmet to protect your head
Otherwise you'll end up
In a casualty bed!

Jack Terrins-Baker (9)
St Patrick's Primary School, Armagh

Weather

Wet and windy,
Dry and cold,
Frosty and icy,
Brings the
Winter snow,
Follow by the
Beautiful colours,
Spring, summer,
And autumn.

Nicole Connolly (9)
St Patrick's Primary School, Armagh

Nature Colours

Red for the roses
Blue for the sky
Green for the grass that grows so high

Yellow for the sun
White for the clouds
Brown for the tree trunks that stand so proud

Black for the night sky
Pink for the shooting stars
Orange for the street lamps held up by metal bars.

Next time it rains and shines
Look up and you'll see the colours of the
Rainbow looking down on me and you.

Emma Toal (8)
St Patrick's Primary School, Armagh

Football

Football, football
I wish I could be
A football star
Just like on TV.

I could play at Highbury
Old Trafford would be great
But as for now
I must watch and wait.

I would play left back
Maybe score a goal or two
Then Fergie would say
My boy! You'll do!

Joshua Loughran (9)
St Patrick's Primary School, Armagh

Fat Frog

Fat frog why are you
Sitting on a log?
Why don't you jump or
Try to jog?

Why are you green, slimy
And fat?
Why don't you play with
The neighbour's cat?

I hear you croak, I watch
You stare.
I wonder what you feel
And care?

You must be happy
Sitting still
Nothing to do but stare
At that window sill.

Oh no! Fat frog
Oh my friend, you've just
Been eaten by that
Hungry, mean old dog!

Luke McSherry (9)
St Patrick's Primary School, Armagh

Winter

Winter, winter,
It's the best
When all the snow comes down to rest.
On the ground it lies so still
Giving Ireland a great chill.
The Robin redbreast is looking for food
And uses his wing as a warm hood.
The hedgehogs are curled up in their nests
Having their long winter rest.

Ciaran Duffy (9)
St Patrick's Primary School, Armagh

Oh Poor Me! My Family

My Dad
My daddy works in Coleraine
He says they should call it ColdRain
With his back he is in great pain
He always does complain
And he's not very happy
He has to go tomorrow again.

My brother
My brother is called Sean
Sometimes he goes on and on
If he doesn't quit
I'll have a blue fit
I've had enough of him.
And that's it!

My baby sister
The baby always does cry
And I can never figure out why
Does she want her dummy,
Or has she got a sore tummy?
I know what to do
Just give her to Mummy.

My Sisters
My sisters always fight
They keep me up at night
I wish they would go to bed
And be quiet for once instead
If they keep this up
I will have a sore head.

Oh poor me! My family.

Damien Gorman (9)
St Patrick's Primary School, Armagh

Smells

I love the smell of Mummy's dinner
As I pass by the house.
I hate the smell of cigarettes
As I hug my Aunty Mo.

I love the smell of sweets
As we give in our charity.
I hate the smell of my dad's feet
Because it makes my heart beat.

I love the smell of Mummy's perfume
As she puts it on my chin.
I hate the smell of my sister's clothes
As she dumps them in a pile.

Lauren McMahon (7)
St Patrick's Primary School, Armagh

Animals

Animals can be big or small
Some are short and some are tall
They can live in woods or underground
There are lots of places where they can be found.
Many are wild but some are tame
Don't you know they're not all the same
The most common pets are dogs and cats
But certainly not bats or rats.
You could keep a goldfish in a bowl
But I don't recommend a mole.

Niall McCoy (9)
St Patrick's Primary School, Armagh

What Is It?

What is it? What is it?
Flying round the night.
What is it? What is it?
A nose shining bright.
It's a reindeer.

What is it? What is it?
It is as green as can be.
What is it? What is it?
It is pretty like me.
It's a Christmas tree.

What is it? What is it?
That goes round a tree.
What is it? What is it?
Oh what could it be?

Why, it is all the presents.

Niamh McKee (8)
St Patrick's Primary School, Armagh

School

If you go to school
You know you're not a fool
You learn something new
Every day
And in between you can play.

You have no time to muck about
For if you do you'll get put out.
Now you know about my school
Where you must obey all the
Rules!

Hannah Pearson (8)
St Patrick's Primary School, Armagh

Smells

I love the smell of hair gel
I hate the smell of a well
I love the smell of a new fluffy mat
I hate the smell of a rat
I love the smell of roast chicken
I hate the smell of burnt toast
I love the smell of me
I hate the smell of salty sea.

Shea McCartney (7)
St Patrick's Primary School, Armagh

Smells

I love the smell of my granny's buns
When I walk into her house.
I love the taste of bubblegum ice cream
When it's cold inside my mouth.
I love the taste of jam doughnuts
When I'm eating them in my mouth.
I hate the smell of Daddy's feet
Because I can smell them from the bedroom.

Natasha Murphy (8)
St Patrick's Primary School, Armagh

Smells

I hate the smell of the salty sea
While walking along the beach.
I love the smell of petrol
At the filling station in town.
I hate the smell of beer
While my uncle's getting drunk.
I love the smell of bacon
When my mummy cooks the dinner.

Rachel Devlin (8)
St Patrick's Primary School, Armagh

Multicoloured Poem

Black house slates glitter in beautiful daylight sun.
I like the look of the slithering red snakes.
Silver plates full of iced topped buns.
Snow-white swans swim in the gleaming lake.

Massive chucking tractors over the drenched green grass.
Purple tulips twist and twirl in the breeze.
The dishwasher can wash the dirty grey glasses.
The hard brown bark on the swaying trees.

Conal Baxter (8)
St Patrick's Primary School, Armagh

Smells And Colours

I love the blue, blue sky, it reminds me of the blue sea.
I love the smell of American fries.
I hate the smell of chicken, it puts me in a bad mood.
I adore red, it's for Tyrone.
I *hate* the smell of my dad's farts
I hate the smell of gas
I *love* multicoloured and smelly things.

Shauna Wilson (7)
St Patrick's Primary School, Armagh

Blue

Blue is the ocean salty water.
Blue is Earth, the planet we live on.
Blue is the sky where the birds fly.
Blue is paint, the colour of my room.
Blue is the colour of my mum's eyes.
Blue is Dublin's flag.
These are colours I adore.

Ben Lavery (7)
St Patrick's Primary School, Armagh

Young Writers - Once Upon A Rhyme Co Armagh

Our Pepper

Pepper is small
Brown and white
We play together every night
He wags his tail
Everyone knows he bites our toes
Just for fun.
He creeps upstairs
And curls up beside me
In the morning
When my mum shouts,
He just pulls the covers
Over his head.
He's ten now and getting old
You'd think he'd have
Learnt to do what he's told.
But he hasn't he's just
Our Pepper.

Claire Hamilton (8)
St Patrick's Primary School, Armagh

Off Sick

Today the cold bug is here
There's nothing else to fear.
My head is sore
My nose is stuffy,
My hair's usually straight
And now it's scruffy.

My stomach's sore
I bang my head,
I feel quite dizzy,
I'll go to bed.

James Devlin (11)
St Patrick's Primary School, Armagh

Multicoloured Poem

I like the multicolours in the world
Because they're bright and colourful.
But when I mix the colours up,
It turns into a muddle.

I love the yellow daffodils fluttering in the wind.
I love the red on the dark red rose,
It's a colour that you could catch.
Blue is the colour of the Dublin flag, as the crowd
Waves them at the match.

I dislike the brown on the bark of the tree,
And the grey of the greedy, creeping rats.
At night when it's dark, I am very, very scared
Because of the big black bats.

Oh please bright colours come back to me
Before it is too *late*.

Jane Toner (8)
St Patrick's Primary School, Armagh

Smells And Multicoloured Poem

I love the colour of the green, green grass.
I hate the smell of gas.
I like the colour of the blue, blue ocean,
The waves bumping up and down.
I adore the smell of lavender,
In my front garden.
I hate the smell of cow dung,
As I pass through the fields on my spring walk
I admire the colour of a pink heart,
On Valentine's Day of course.

Hannah McCann (8)
St Patrick's Primary School, Armagh

Be Safe Be Seen

At night you need to be bright
Cars go by and they can see ahead
You need to be careful
Or you could be dead
That's not so funny
If you're no longer alive
Be careful at night
And be sure to be bright
Fluorescent strips are sure to be seen
They gleam at cars
For hours and hours
So wear bright clothes
Be sure to be seen
Lights on your bike are good
So if you go out tonight
Be sure you're alert and bright.

Cathal McArdle (11)
St Patrick's Primary School, Armagh

Smell

I hate the smell of my dog
I like the smell of fizzy lemonade
I hate the smell of raw onions
They always make me cry
I love the smell of apple pie
But the worst smell is cigarettes
My favourite smell is air freshener with the
Lovely smell of red apples.

Lauren Pattison (8)
St Patrick's Primary School, Armagh

Be Safe Be Seen

Every day we are reminded
Of the dangers on the road,
Drivers and pedestrians
Are urged to obey the code.

Speed can be a killer
And many lives are lost,
By people taking chances
To pay an awful cost.

When walking wear an armband,
Especially at night.
Drivers then will see you
If you are wearing something bright.
When crossing a road,
Look right, left, right again,
And if there is no traffic
Cross over, only then.

When driving, wear a seatbelt,
It well may save your life,
Or the lives of many children,
A husband or a wife.

Let everyone be reminded
To obey the golden rules,
Let's have happy motoring,
Without the driving fools.

Niamh McMahon (10)
St Patrick's Primary School, Armagh

Easter

Easter, Easter
Is so much fun
We eat and we eat
Until our bellies are full.

Big eggs, small eggs
Brown eggs and white eggs
With Smarties and Skittles
We eat all night.
That's such a delight.

Nicole Mallon (11)
St Patrick's Primary School, Armagh

Off Sick

I wish I was dead but I'm just in my bed
Sick as can be oh why me?
My tummy aches and I can't enjoy any cakes.
My mum says I'm ill as she hands me a pill.
I only have the energy to sleep,
But I want to get outside
But all I can do is peep.

Declan Donnelly (10)
St Patrick's Primary School, Armagh

I Wish

I wish I was more pretty, I wish I had a baby brother or sister.
I wish I lived in a big city, walk around the city without getting
a blister.
I wish I didn't have to get up early.
I wish I didn't have to eat a curly wurly.
I wish I didn't have to fold my clothes.
I wish I didn't have to blow my nose.

Sophie Knipe (11)
St Patrick's Primary School, Armagh

All The World Is A Book

All the world is a book
The men and women each day turn a page
The children too.
Page one is the baby's 1st Birthday, 1st word, 1st steps.
Page two is focused on childhood; 1st day at Primary School,
1st day at Secondary School.
Page three the teenage years; passing driving test,
going to university.
Page four the young adult; first job, moving out.
Page five the adult; fortieth birthday, growing older.
Page six the elder; getting crippled, doctor's help.
Page seven death; lose sight, lose taste, lose smell,
lose hearing, lose feeling, lose life.

Lauren Devlin (10)
St Patrick's Primary School, Armagh

Be Safe Be Seen

Be safe be seen is the rule
Follow the rules and be cool
Don't be a fool and follow the rules
Look both ways when crossing the road
Don't run, don't go too slow
Don't race at tremendous pace
Walk normally, carefully and safely
If you are going out at night
Make sure you wear something bright.
When crossing the road don't be a fool
Remember the golden safety rule.

Nicole Reilly (11)
St Patrick's Primary School, Armagh

A Day Off School

Day off school
May sound cool
But you get bored
It may rain or snow
And there is
Nowhere
to go
So you stay inside and
hide,
remember
A day off school may sound
cool
but it's not.

Aoife McVeigh (11)
St Patrick's Primary School, Armagh

Sam's Coming Home

They are heading for Armagh
We are going to cheer them on
People are saying to the bus driver,
Please hoot the horn.

Armagh has won Sam again
Tyrone are on their own
Armagh are training really hard
Tyrone will have a groan.

Armagh's keeping Sam
Tyrone can keep their crystal,
Armagh and Tyrone are back to back
They'll shoot out like a pistol.

Shannon McKeown (11)
St Patrick's Primary School, Armagh

Sound Poem

I love the sound of silence.
I love the sound of birds singing.
And when we go past the sea, it smells so beautiful as
the waves splash against the stony walls.
I love when babies breathe in their sleep.
I love the screeching of the fans when *Armagh* won the
All Ireland.
I hate the sound of dogs barking.
I do not like the sound of children crying.
I do not like my mummy snoring and talking in her sleep.
It means that I am wide awake.
I hate children yelling in the yard.

Niamh Cauldwell (8)
St Patrick's Primary School, Armagh

Smell

I like the smell of the chips
I love the smell of the crispy dips
I adore the smell of the daffodils
Pushing up in the spring.
I hate the smell of cows dung
I detest the smell of the petrol in my car.
I extremely dislike the smell of smoke coming
from a fire
But the smell I really hate the most is the
smell of my uncle's cigars.

Tiarnan McArdle (8)
St Patrick's Primary School, Armagh

When I Was Sick

Feeling hot and sticky, groggy and out of sorts.
I'm really under the weather, I think
I'm going to puke.

I really am off colour and feeling unwell
The room has started spinning
I think I am going to throw *up!*

Chloe Mulholland (11)
St Patrick's Primary School, Armagh

Sound

I love the sound of the bees buzzing
I love the sound of the cracking of thunder and lightning.
My favourite one is the bird singing in the sky.
I hate the sound of the mice squeaking all night long.
I don't like dogs barking.
I definitely don't like when my daddy wakes me up
In the morning to go to school.

Maria McGee (8)
St Patrick's Primary School, Armagh

Sound

I love the sound of rain as it drips down the drain.
I adore the sound of splashing through puddles on a winter's day.
My favourite sound is the leaves twirling down from the trees.
I also enjoy the sound of rulers cracking.
I hate the sound of children crunching through the leaves.
I dislike when my cousin Ruairi snores.

Shannagh Skipsey (8)
St Patrick's Primary School, Armagh

Winter

In the winter nothing can grow
Because of the snow.
Sometimes when it is snowy,
It might also be blowy.
When the lake begins to freeze,
There may also be a breeze.
Mum said, 'Chickens on the boil.'
But soon the oven ran out of oil.
We wear warm clothes when it blows
And also when it snows.
The shorter the days and longer the nights,
The more the children have snowball fights.
Some animals sleep
But some don't like the sheep.

Maeve Mulholland (8)
St Patrick's Primary School, Lurgan

Winter

In winter our house is heated by oil
The birds cannot eat out of the soil.
We eat lots of meat
As we warm our feet.
We wear warm woolly clothes
When outside it snows.
Plants and grass cannot grow
As it starts to snow.
In the day we like to play
We can make a little sleigh.
We have lots of snowball fights
As it gets to longer nights.

Nuala McMahon (7)
St Patrick's Primary School, Lurgan

Young Writers - Once Upon A Rhyme Co Armagh

Winter

In winter there is a chilly breeze
That might make you freeze.
No plants grow
When it starts to snow.
We wear boots on our feet
When we're walking on the sleet.
The best thing about winter is the
Snowball fights
When children are playing in the nights.

Niall McDowell (7)
St Patrick's Primary School, Lurgan

Winter

In winter it might be very snowy
Or very, very blowy.
Some animals might sleep
All except the woolly sheep.
We always like snowball fights
But not in the cold nights.
Every day the children play
On the bright red sleigh.

Ciáran Coleman (8)
St Patrick's Primary School, Lurgan

Winter

In winter most animals go to sleep
Except for sheep.
You would be sensible to wear woolly clothes
When the icy wind blows.
We eat meat
When we go out in the sleet.

Niall Kerr (8)
St Patrick's Primary School, Lurgan

Winter

In winter the farmer puts the sheep in the shed
And they go to bed.
We wear warm clothes
When it snows.
When it does snow
It sometimes will blow.
My house is heated by oil
But the moles are in the soil.
The snow falls
In balls.
I eat warm foods
And then I go to snooze.
Flowers die
And the birds can't fly.
Let's go and play
On my sleigh today.

Ciara Corrigan (7)
St Patrick's Primary School, Lurgan

Winter

In winter it is very snowy
But sometimes it is very blowy.
Some animals go to sleep
But not the sheep.
Every day the children play
On the bright red sleigh.
When there's not a breeze
The ground starts to freeze
But when there's a breeze
The ground doesn't freeze.
Our house is heated by oil
And birds can't get anything to
Eat from the soil.

Tony Mulligan (8)
St Patrick's Primary School, Lurgan

My Winter Poem

Winter, winter,
Is here again.
Children playing in the snow,
Everywhere I go.
Having fun,
As they run.
Throwing snowballs,
Making snowmen.
But best of all,
Is lying down
In the cold and freezing snow.
With arms and legs outstretched
Do I dare?
Stay so long,
To move my arms and legs
And make cool angels
In the snow.

Claire McCone (9)
St Teresa's Primary School, Mountnorris

My Poem About Christmas Eve

Nearly midnight still can't sleep!
Has he been yet?
Dare I peep?
Sneak out softly, creaking floor!
Down the stairs and through the door . . .
In the darkness by the tree, tightly wrapped . . . but which
For me.

Tracey McSherry (8)
St Teresa's Primary School, Mountnorris

Dull Day

It's wet, it's dull, can't go out to play
It's been a misty foggy day.
It's January cold and drowsy
It makes us all feel pretty lousy.
The lights are on with a blazing fire
Sitting in the house is so much drier.
Watching TV visitors here,
It's really not such a bad time of year.
Sometimes we have snow, the cars go slow,
We look like goats, wrapped up in coats.

Natasha Hamilton (9)
St Teresa's Primary School, Mountnorris

Colour Change

Up at our farm
All looks different
We go to spread slurry
But the field is
White with frost
It seems such a pity
To turn such lovely
Silvery-white
To brown.

Gareth Feenan (10)
St Teresa's Primary School, Mountnorris

Summer

I love summer because it's nice and hot.
I can go out and play without getting wet.
I can sit outside and have a tasty picnic.
And get lots of lollies to lick and lick and lick.
I can go to the beach and play in the sea.
And have a lovely day, my family and me.

Brendan O'Hare (7)
St Teresa's Primary School, Mountnorris

Bob

I have a tiny reindeer,
He says his name is Bob.
He likes to entertain me,
He says that is his job.
I like it when Bob juggles,
Or plays the drum for me.
Sometimes we sing together,
And sometimes we have tea.
My brother doesn't believe
In my tiny reindeer friend.
He says there's no such reindeer,
But why would Bob pretend.

Tanith Nesbitt (9)
St Teresa's Primary School, Mountnorris

My Winter Poem

I hear the wind is blowing strong,
The nights are darker and very long.
The snow is lying on the ground,
Children playing all around.

I built a snowman, he is really white.
Then I enjoyed a snowball fight.
My mummy lights the log fire,
Will it clear the fog?
The moon and stars come out at night,
Oh what a beautiful sight.

Julie McSherry (8)
St Teresa's Primary School, Mountnorris

Winter

Winter,
Winter
Is here,
The fires are being lit
And the snow is falling
Thick and white.
The children are having fun
Gloves, hats and scarves
Are being knitted,
And Jack Frost is out and about.
The end.

Seamus Toher (11)
St Teresa's Primary School, Mountnorris

Winter Likes

Winter woolly scarves
Bright lights in the quays
Sitting on the floor
A blazing fire
Pots of hot soup and stew
Watching Mary Poppins on TV
Walking up to Granny's in the frost
Playing with my cousins
Cathal telling jokes.
That's what I like about winter.

Zoe Carr (9)
St Teresa's Primary School, Mountnorris

A Winter's Morning

When you go outside,
On a winter's morning.
You may slip and slide,
While the ice just glistens.

I'll call up all my friends,
And we shall play all of today.
Hoping today never ends,
Because today is so much fun.

Lauren O'Hare (9)
St Teresa's Primary School, Mountnorris

I Saw A Poor Crying Dolphin At The Circus

This dolphin wants to be free,
And jump about with the other dolphins in the sea,
The dolphin doesn't like running the show,
It prefers most other dolphins flow.

The dolphin is balancing a ball on its nose,
It says to itself 'I hate this pose,'
The dolphin is getting very afraid,
But now the crowd is starting to fade.

The dolphin starts to move about,
It really, really wants to get out,
She, the dolphin is going out of line,
The dolphin is letting out a depressing whine.

The dolphin is starting to cry,
And what I just said was not a lie,
I jump and try to save her,
The circus clown asks 'What are you doing Sir?'

Conan Hoey (9)
Seagoe Primary School

My Sister Saw A Swimming Seal

My sister saw a swimming seal
In the zoo one summer day.
The seal swam with glass and litter,
And hoop and ball to jump through.

And the seal swam up without a sound
And jumped through the hoop in the summer heat
The people laughed and shouted to see it all
And the seal gazed at all the people in the heat.

The keeper standing at the entrance
Standing with a cup and hat,
The seal gazed out in the open
Seeing the food and waves in the distance.

Shannon Cambell (10)
Seagoe Primary School

Hope

Hope is as white as snow,
Hope smells like a sweet rose.
It tastes warm and fresh,
It sounds like soft music.
Hope feels like a soft sheet of cotton,
Hope lives in the heart of a flower.

Linzi Maxwell (9)
Seagoe Primary School

Hate

Hate is a dark deep red,
And it smells like sweaty armpits,
It tastes just like earwax,
It sounds like howling wolves,
And it feels as hard as a rock,
It lives in a very dark cave.

Zoe Hagan (10)
Seagoe Primary School

My Brother Saw A Lonely Gorilla

My brother saw a lonely gorilla
At the zoo one day,
He stood up at the window sill
Not even wanting to play.

He walks right round his window sill
With nothing for him to do,
He looks so sad
And he's just a wee lad, with nothing to do.

I cam imagine him now
Out in the wild,
With his mother
And her wonderful child.

Being free in the jungle
Is a wonderful thing,
Right now
To hear the birds sing.

Holly Rathore (9)
Seagoe Primary School

Anger

Anger is red.
It smells like plastic smouldering
It tastes like burnt toast,
It sounds like bombs going off
It feels like a sharp dagger
It lives in the dumps.

Jason Webb (10)
Seagoe Primary School

My Dad Saw A Crying Gorilla

My dad saw a crying gorilla,
At the zoo one day.
He saw the tears dripping down his soft gentle face.

The gorilla had to do a dance.
You could see his aching eyes crying away,
And the burning sun shining down on his back.

What did the gorilla get for a reward?
He got a round of applause,
And he went in, back in his cage
The poor lonely thing.

Jessica Gilpin (10)
Seagoe Primary School

Death

Death is as black as darkness,
It smells like rotten coal in the fire,
Death tastes like dirt on the ground,
It sounds like people screeching as loud as they can,
It feels like a sharp dagger cutting through your body.
Death lives underground.

Jonathan Beattie (10)
Seagoe Primary School

Jealousy

Jealousy is green
It smells of mouldy cheese,
Jealousy tastes like a bitter lemon
It's nails clawing on a blackboard,
It's spiky and rough
Jealousy lives in a dark, damp cupboard.

Katy McComb (9)
Seagoe Primary School

Jealousy

Jealousy is dark red,
Its smell is rotten eggs,
Jealousy tastes like sour grapes,
It sounds like a shrieking cry,
Jealousy feels like thorns and needles,
And it lives in a dark forgotten forest.

Serena Christie (9)
Seagoe Primary School

Excitement

Excitement is bright red,
And it smells like a citrus candle
It's the taste of a chocolate sprinkled ice cream
And it sounds like children laughing.
It feels like snowflakes touching my hand.
Excitement's home is in a garden of flowers.

Esther Hewitt (9)
Seagoe Primary School

Happiness

Happiness is red
It is the smell of a chocolate cake
And it tastes like fresh, sweet, strawberries,
Happiness sounds like a baby giggling
It feels soft and smooth
And happiness lives in a place full of trees and flowers.

Jordan Ritchie (9)
Seagoe Primary School

Happiness

Happiness is yellow
It smells like a bunch of flowers,
And it tastes like a fresh fruit salad.
Happiness sounds like children laughing and playing,
It feels like a rabbit's soft coat.
Happiness lives in the first lamb in spring.

Hannah Forsythe (10)
Seagoe Primary School

Kindness

Kindness is lime green
It smells of homemade apple pie,
Kindness tastes like raspberry yoghurt
It sounds like a lullaby playing on the flute.
Kindness feels as smooth as rabbit's fur
And it lives in a soft, comfy chair.

Hayley Cullen (9)
Seagoe Primary School

War

Dark brown is the colour of war
It smells of rusty metal,
War tastes like bitter lemons
And is the sound of deafening bombs,
It's like rubbing rough wood along your hands
War lives in a dark alley.

Michael Busby (10)
Seagoe Primary School

War

War is blood red.
It smells like the smoke of burning forests.
War tastes like charred meat.
It sounds like a bomb exploding.
It feels rough.
War lives in a dark cave.

Richard Carson (10)
Seagoe Primary School

War

War is black
It smells of wood burning
War has the taste of sour milk
The sound is bombs dropping
It feels rough and hard
War lives in a field of dead flowers.

Lauren Anderson (10)
Seagoe Primary School

Cruelty

Cruelty is dark purple
Dead corpses is the smell,
Blood is the iron taste of cruelty
It sounds like a victorious bully laughing,
Stinging nettles feel cruel
An ice cold heart is its evil lair.

Mark Scott (9)
Seagoe Primary School

Cruelty

Cruelty is black
Blazing forests smell of cruelty
Its taste is burnt toast
Cruelty is a baby's scream
It feels like prickly thorns
An abandoned building is its home.

David Busby (10)
Seagoe Primary School

Luck

Luck is yellow
It smells like freshly squeezed oranges
The taste of luck is a strawberry cut in half with sugar,
Luck sounds like laughter
It feels like velvet
And it lives in a field of daffodils.

Lindsey Stevenson (10)
Seagoe Primary School

Death

Death is black
It's the smell of smoke coming from a fire
Sour cream is the taste of death,
People screaming for help sounds like death
It feels very rocky and crunchy
Death lives in a graveyard.

Rhys Harris (10)
Seagoe Primary School

Peace

Peace is violet
The smell is like a lavender scented candle
Peace tastes like juicy grapes,
Peace sounds like a gentle breeze
It feels so soft and smooth
Peace lives in a golden heart.

Beth Wright (9)
Seagoe Primary School

Peace

Peace is pale blue
And it smells like fresh bread out of an oven.
Its taste is melted chocolate and marshmallows.
Peace is the sound of a harp
And peace is as smooth as silk.
Peace lives in a field of poppies.

Christine Bell (9)
Seagoe Primary School

Love

Love is red
It smells of strawberries
Love tastes of a Dairy Milk chocolate drink,
Its sound is soft romantic music
Love feels like smooth velvet
Love lives in the heart of flowers.

Hannah Todd (9)
Seagoe Primary School

Winter Recipe

Crisp a bowl of grass,
Season with dead leaves,
Knead in some hard brown soil.

Mix in some frozen icicles,
Sprinkle in a little snow,
And the rind of a snowflake.

Stir in the juice of a yellow moon,
Sieve in a pinch of stars,
And cover for two days.

Decorate with snowballs,
Harden for three months,
And you have made winter.

Jonathan Hilliard (11)
Seagoe Primary School

Love

Love is heart warming pink
A fresh rose is its scent
It tastes like strawberries and cream,
The sound of love is soft, romantic music
Love feels like a warm teddy bear
And love lives in your heart.

Lily Robinson (9)
Seagoe Primary School

Winter Recipe

Take the cold breeze,
White snow mixed with frost,
Golden leaves and bare trees.

Mix them all together,
Then take a sieve to drain any water,
And leave to set.

Sprinkle the powder over,
Until nicely covered,
Then add a touch of icing.

Leave on the side,
With tinfoil on it,
Put in your freezer for three months.

Sarah Clifford (10)
Seagoe Primary School

Winter Window

Dancing across the ice the fairies of snow
Were out last night
Creating a winter wonderland
Outside my winter window.

A robin hops, seeking for food
While trying to keep warm
Outside my winter window.

The snow begins to fall again
The brisk wind howls through the leafless trees
Outside my winter window.

Gillian Bell (11)
Seagoe Primary School

Winter Window

Gleaming frost on the ground,
Like fairies dancing around,
Through my winter window.

Silver lining, shimmering brightly,
The fairies movement getting lighter,
Through my winter window.

Fairies leave, no more dancing,
The night dies down
Through my winter window.

Rebekah Wallace (11)
Seagoe Primary School

My Phone, My Dog, Blue Birds

My Phone
I hate my phone
Well I hate the ring tone
It is a pain to me
So I get a cane to whip it
And throw a pip at it!

My Dog
My dog is big
She is a pig
When she went outside
She did not know where to hide.

Blue birds
Blue birds are pink
And pink birds are blue
And I do not know where to blink
Or wink, pink, pink.

Kirsten Doran (7)
The Armstrong Primary School

What Is Orange?

Orange is a volcano
Exploding at night.
Orange is a fire
Burning light and bright.
Orange is a sunset
At Ibiza so light.
Orange is a tiger
Fierce as can be.
Orange is a heartburn
Sore and long.
Orange is the sand
Hot and smooth.
Orange is a bright idea
Clever as can be.
Orange is the summer sun
Hot as can be.

Rebecca Loney (8)
The Armstrong Primary School

Wind

When the wind blows gates creak,
Doors clatter
When the wind blows,
Curtains swish, paper scatters.

When the wind blows
The street lights mutter
When the wind blows
The leaves flutter and the twigs mutter.

Chloe Wilson (7)
The Armstrong Primary School

What Is Blue?

Blue is the sky
So beautiful and light.
Blue is the sea
So playful at night.
Blue is your uniform
So warm and cosy.
Blue is a waterfall
So lovely and rocky.
Blue is a dolphin
That swims underwater.
Blue is blu-tac
So sticky and stretchy.
Blue is a tie
So long and triangular.
Blue is jeans
So stripy and rough.

Nathan Beatty (8)
The Armstrong Primary School

What Is Red?

Red are the leaves
That fly in the sky.
Red is a pencil case
Flopping around.
Red is a lunchbox
Who ate all the lunch?
Red is a helicopter
That makes a big noise.
Red is a word book
That has the alphabet.

Matthew Blair (7)
The Armstrong Primary School

What Is Green?

Green is a jumper woolly and warm
Green is a lizard scaly but small
Green is a lettuce leafy and fat
Green is a snake long and smooth
Green is a leaf thin and flat
Green is a car loud and wide
Green is a train as fast as can be
Green is a dragon an animal so strong
Green is a crocodile thin and long.

Clive Knipe (8)
The Armstrong Primary School

What Is Green?

Green are leaves that flutter in the sky.
Green are frogs all sticky and slimy.
Green are grapes all juicy and gorgeous.
Green is a hedge all prickly and spiky.
Green is grass all long and itchy.
Green are cars all fast and running.

Philip Gordon (8)
The Armstrong Primary School

What Is White?

White is snow soft, cold and wet.
White is a polar bear so fluffy
and puffy.
White is a sheep all woolly and warm.
White is a tissue, so, so soft.
White is a seagull noisy and greedy.
White is chalk, hard and lots of dust.

Cara Best (8)
The Armstrong Primary School

What Is White?

White is the snowman
Big as a tree
White is a scarf
As long as a ruler,
White is the sock
That is smelly and warm
White is a door
As hard as a book,
White is a card
So giant and wide
White is the snow
As slippery as the floor.

Jessie Kwok (7)
The Armstrong Primary School

What Is Blue?

Blue is the sea
Happy as can be.
Blue is your uniform
Woolly and warm.
Blue is the sky
Beautiful and light.
Blue is a whale
As big as a tail.
Blue is a crayon
Round and smooth.
Blue is a door
A rectangle shape.

Alan Humphries (7)
The Armstrong Primary School

What Is Black?

Black is a shoe so dark and dull.
Black is a sky on a rainy day.
Black is sin.
Black is ink.
Black is a pen so good at writing.
Black is a cauldron for spells
And things.
Black is a bin bag so stretchy
And smooth.

Jason Burt (8)
The Armstrong Primary School

What Is Green?

Green is the grass long as can be
Green is the trees covered in leaves
And maybe a green, green
Cactus so prickly.
Green is a newt so cold and wet.
Green is the colour of sick that
Is *horrible*
Green are the peas that I like eating.

Laura Isted (7)
The Armstrong Primary School

What Is Blue?

Blue is the sea salty as can be
Blue is a pencil, long and thin,
Sometimes as thin as a pin.
Blue is a wall long and tall
Blue is a flower beautiful and pretty
Blue is a car that goes very fast,
One that will last.

Hannah McClure (7)
The Armstrong Primary School

What Is Yellow?

Yellow is the bright stars that shine in the sky.
Yellow is the hot dangerous fire.
Yellow is a rough fierce lion.
Yellow is the sun which is very bright and strong.
Yellow is a giraffe very very tall.
It has such big long legs.
Yellow is the sand dusty and bright.
Yellow is a bruise which looks very sore.
Yellow is a duck that says quack, quack, quack.

Lisa Murray (8)
The Armstrong Primary School

What Is Green?

Green is a frog all sticky and slimy.
Green is a jumper all woolly and warm.
Green is the grass all leathery and strong.
Green is a leaf blowing in the wind.
Green is a pear all musty inside.
When you feel sick green tingles inside you.
Green is a grape all juicy inside.

Madeleine Armstrong (8)
The Armstrong Primary School

The Sun Is . . .

The sun is a gold coin in the air
It is a beach ball kicked in the air
It is a circular yellow cushion
It is a yellow football
It is a gold bottle cap.

Robert Armstrong (9)
The Armstrong Primary School

What Is . . . The Moon

The moon is like a silver coin
You always use to buy things
The moon is like a thumb print
On a dark piece of paper
The moon is like a round white diamond
You wear for a wedding
The moon is like a big sphere
You learn in shapes
The moon is like a football
You kick about in the day
The moon is like the sun
In the morning when it comes out.

Stephanie Chan (10)
The Armstrong Primary School

What Is Blue?

Blue is the sea calm and wavy.
Blue is a pencil long and sharp.
Blue is a jumper lovely and warm.
Blue are boots mucky and new.
Blue is a wall huge and big.
Blue is for rubber smooth and handy.
Blue is for a car big and long.
Blue is for books thick and thin.

Robert Davidson (8)
The Armstrong Primary School

The Moon Is . . .

The moon is a big lump of cheese
The moon is a big football
The moon is a head
The moon is a sphere
The moon is a nice pillow.

James Neville (10)
The Armstrong Primary School

What Is . . . The Snow?

The snow is feathers falling from a
pillow in the sky.
The snow is a very small ice cream
falling from the sky.
The snow is white paint on the biggest
ever sheet of black paper
The snow is a cotton wool ball
drifting in the night
The snow is a glistening carpet
underneath the street lights.

Claire Gilmore (10)
The Armstrong Primary School

What Is Snow?

Snow is a falling star,
Snow is a small fluffy cloud falling from the sky.
It is bits of paper ripped up.
It is a white fingerprint,
Snow is lots of ping-pong balls,
And snow is lots of fun!

Ashleigh Kerr (9)
The Armstrong Primary School

What Is . . . Frost?

Frost is like vanilla ice cream at the top of a hill,
Frost is like tiny icicles dangling across the roof,
It is like smoke, but doesn't move,
It is like silver lipstick spread *everywhere*
Frost is like silver ballet dancers skating across the ice.

Emily Colvin (10)
The Armstrong Primary School

What Is The Rainbow?

The rainbow that I see is colourful
Strips of eye shadow.
It is strips of coloured paper
It's a bridge of lovely colours
It is an upside down smile.
But most of all it's a . . .
Rainbow.

Kelly McNeilly (10)
The Armstrong Primary School

What Is Ice?

Ice is a sheet of glass
Ice is a window
Ice is a sheet of tin foil
Ice is a slippery banana skin
Ice is freezing cold water
Ice is still dark water.

Timmy Hassard (9)
The Armstrong Primary School

What Is . . . The Moon?

The moon is a roll of cheese
The moon is a yellow thumb print on black card
The moon is a bright illumination
The moon is golden hair
The moon is a golden coin
That is what the moon is like!

Alice Bingham (10)
The Armstrong Primary School

Seasons

Spring is the time of year
When everything
Is new and clear
It is the New Year.

Summer is on the beach
Making sandcastles and going swimming
It is hot not cold
We will stay here until autumn's here.

Autumn is when leaves are falling
The wind is whirling and the leaves are twirling
Hedgehogs and squirrels hibernate
For winter is very near.

Winter is here, snow, ice and sleet
Comes in winter,
Perfect for children
Bad for adults.
The year's almost over, oh dear!

Ethan Ross (8)
The Armstrong Primary School

What Is . . . Singing?

Singing is the wind blowing in the night
and birds singing in the morning.
Singing is the dogs howling and the
wolves doing the same.
Singing is a bee buzzing all around
and all day through until the night comes around.
Singing is raindrops falling on the rooftops
and little boys splashing around in the puddles.

Lindsey Smyth (9)
The Armstrong Primary School

Winter

Winter is good
Winter is fun
It's the best for everyone
Snow comes down, snow melts
Come out and have some fun.
Let's have snowball fights
Come on everyone,
Let's build an igloo, no let's build a snowman
For all to see.
Put on the hat, put on the eyes,
Don't forget about the scarf.
Oh no! the snow is melting.
Rush, rush into the house,
We need to get in before we get wet.
Goodbye snowman, for another year.

Dean Symington (9)
The Armstrong Primary School

Rabbits

Rabbits are very nice,
I like them very much
But sometimes they can bite,
So please watch out if you have one.
They have very big teeth,
Crunch, crunch, crunch, goes the rabbit
Eating his big carrot.
They have big fluffy tails,
Like a big fluffy ball.
Hop, hop, hop round the dining room.
I wish I had one at my house
So please get me one.

Emma Blaney (9)
The Armstrong Primary School

Dalmatians

D otty, oh so dotty
A ll sorts of sizes
L ovely little spots
M any different prizes
A ll so cuddly
T wo hundred and one
I wish I had one as my buddy
A h they are so fun
N ever had one
S o, so many, must have one.

Kerry-Anne Wright (9)
The Armstrong Primary School

Winter

Snow is really great,
I play with my mate,
And I love playing with snowballs
When snow falls.

I like building snowmen,
With my friend Ben.
In winter there is ice,
And it is very nice.

Rosalind McClean (8)
The Armstrong Primary School

Chickens

I think chickens are rather nice,
But I think they taste like mice.
Chickens are orange, chickens are yellow,
Chickens have no chins at all.
Chickens, chickens, chickens are nice
But chickens don't smell very nice.

Kylie Tucker (8)
The Armstrong Primary School

What Is Gold?

Gold is a colour
Fit for a king.
Gold is an earring
Cool for boys.
A pound coin is gold
Good for saving
Gold is a watch
'What time is it?'
Ring is a marriage
Isn't it nice?
Gold medals
Given out on sports day.
Lots of gold jewels
Fit for a queen.

Scott Armstrong (8)
The Armstrong Primary School

Ponies

I have a pony
She's called Leonie,
We go riding together
On her saddle leather.

Her breed is Shetland
We trot along the sand
I wear my boots
My hard hat and jodhpurs.

I muck out the stable
With a broom
And then I start to groom,
That's why I like ponies.

Hannah McCann (9)
The Armstrong Primary School

Cars

Cars are fast speedy things
Cars are cool and sporty
Oh! I might have broken my back
Racing round the windy track.
So, so fast
I fly past 6,
I'm nearly finished,
I don't give up
I've won the race.

Michael Hoey (9)
The Armstrong Primary School

Chinchillas

Chinchillas, chinchillas
Fluffy little creatures
So many different sizes
So many different colours
Very sharp teeth they might bite,
Buy me, buy me one please!

Sarah Stewart (8)
The Armstrong Primary School

Football

I like playing football
It is so fun
It makes me run
I can win the ball
It is so fun
I like running about
Come on, it is so fun.

Michael Dobbs (9)
The Armstrong Primary School

Dogs

I like dogs
They are fluffy
They run around the garden
And get so muddy
There's different kinds
Small and big,
I love dogs,
They are great.

Danielle Sutcliffe (9)
The Armstrong Primary School

Dogs

I love dogs
They are very cuddly
They get so muddy
But I don't mind
Dogs are so kind
Big or small
But dogs are really great!

Jane Oliver (8)
The Armstrong Primary School

What Is A Rainbow?

A rainbow is a sad, sad face,
It is a colourful bridge
It is party streamers straightened across the sky
It is a circle out in half,
It is bright and beautiful lines
Curved across the blue sky.

Josh Finlay (10)
The Armstrong Primary School

What Is Yellow?

Yellow is lightning
Knocking down trees.
Yellow is soda
Popping out of a jar.
Yellow is the glory of Christ the Lord
Because of the light of Jesus.
Yellow is a star lying in the sky
Blazing with the light of the moon
Shiny as can be
Yellow, Yellow, Yellow.

Simon Watson (7)
The Armstrong Primary School

What Is Red?

Red is a rug
Snug as a bug.
Red is a ribbon
Lovely as can be.
Red is a thread
Blood if you're dead.
Red is a ball
Very, very small.
Red is a light
Very, very bright.

Emma McNeilly (7)
The Armstrong Primary School

What Is Black?

Black is a fast motorbike.
Black is a skunk that stinks a lot.
Black is a black painted USA rocket
Black is coke going fizzy wizzy.

Adam Marshall (7)
The Armstrong Primary School

What Is Red?

Red is the colour
Of sparkling hair.
Red is the colour
Of a crayon without fear.
Red is the colour
Of a football shirt.
Red is the colour
Of paint so bright.
Red is the colour
Of a felt-tip pen.
Red is the colour
Of a rose with a busy bee inside.
Red is the colour
Of a pencil from Woolworths.
Red is the colour
Of a car with a shower.
Red is the colour of an old raggedy carpet.
Red is the colour of blood so stingy.

Christopher Gillespie (8)
The Armstrong Primary School

What Is Blue?

Blue is a colour
It's cold alright.
Blue's a penguin's favourite colour.
With its blue bobble hat.
Blue's a sky
Where angels fly.
Blue is a blue bird
Flying so high.
Blue is my lunch box
Mmmm . . . mmm
Blue is my schoolbag
To put my books in.

Ellen Donaldson (8)
The Armstrong Primary School

What Is Blue?

Blue is the sky
With the clouds so bright.
Wise blue eyes
Like a river lies.
Blue is raindrops
That always go pop!
Blue is the sea
Rather salty for me.
Blue is the pool
Always nice and cool.
Blue is our school uniform
I'm wearing today.
Blue is the river
That runs through the town.
And I think blue
Is like a clown.

Claire Hanna (8)
The Armstrong Primary School

What Is Red?

Red is blood
That runs through your veins.
Red is a ladybird
On a leaf.
Red is a fire
Burning hot.
Red is a brick
For a house.
Red is the colour
Of Santa's suit.

William Gillanders (8)
The Armstrong Primary School

What Is Blue?

Blue is the sea,
On a sunny day.
Blue is the sky
Can we go out to play?
Blue is our uniform so
Lovely and warm.
But all I have is worn.

Sophie Gillespie (8)
The Armstrong Primary School

The Seaside

The crabs click their pincers
While the fish swish in the sea,
And the children play happily
The sun is shining, so get lotion on,
And sing a jolly old song.
It's time to go home after an exciting day,
So I'll see you again on the beach.

Ellen Coulter (10)
The Cope Primary School

My Mouse

My mouse is brown,
Fat and cheeky,
It likes to eat carrots,
It sleeps in a rabbit hutch and,
Bounces about all night,
I think she's like a rabbit
The way she acts all day.

Rebecca Reid (8)
The Cope Primary School

My Dad

Rugby lover
Golf player
Maths wizard
11+ freak
Funny person
Movie mad
Good laugh
Cool dude
Meat merchant
Fast driver.

James Hewitt (10)
The Cope Primary School

My Dog

Food lover
Tomato hater
Cat catcher
Bone sucker
Teddy ripper
Stone catcher
Ground sniffer
Tale wagger.

Jenny Blevins (11)
The Cope Primary School

Winter

Winter is frosty
Winter is cold
Winter is white
You get frostbite.

Richard Allen (11)
The Cope Primary School

JD

Walk lover
Fast eater
Sleepy head
Quick runner
Cat catcher
Good swimmer
Football player
Fierce barker
Bone chewer
Water drinker
Very frisky.

Stephen Hook (10)
The Cope Primary School

A Good Friend

Golf king
Poem whizz
Can't sing!
Loves Fizz
PlayStation lover
English master
Friendly person
Always faster.

Lee Coleman (10)
The Cope Primary School

Maths Whizz!

There was a young fellow called Ben,
Who's favourite number was ten,
And when it came to maths,
His result was always a pass,
He wrote in invisible pen!

David McKennell (11)
The Cope Primary School

The Terrible Twos

Our house is filled with loudness
From break of dawn till dusk,
Because my two-year-old sister likes
To make a lot of fuss,
To start the day at 7am
The toys come crashing out,
Some banging,
Some clanking,
Thumping,
And knocking,
Oh what a hullabaloo!

The constant commotion is ear-splitting
No doubt,
The house is soundless when she's not about,
The worst time is us having tea,
She sits and roars
Especially at me,
She doesn't drink her milk,
She doesn't eat her tea,
That's when Dad starts shouting to
Gobble up her meal,
But the uproar sounds again when she
Has to go to bed.
And the only way it ends is to let her
Hold her ted.
Everyone talks about the terrible twos,
But wait till they meet Kate
She's real bad news!

Christine Crawford (11)
The Cope Primary School

Holidays

I love to go on holidays, it is my favourite thing
Staying in the sun until I get really warm.

I would burn and burn and burn but I don't really care,
Staying in the sun is the best thing on Earth.

I would always go to Spain, there's lot of stuff to do
I always wake my mum and say 'Come on!'

I run and jump into the pool, I act like it's really cool
I swim and swim all day long
Until it's three o'clock.

Then I go to look around the shops really late at night
When I get back at midnight I go and see the shows.

I go to bed about one o'clock when my dad starts to snore.
I never get to sleep
With the loud loud noise.

Anna Ritchie (10)
The Cope Primary School

Spring

Brighter mornings and milder days
Flowers start blooming in radiant ways
Blossom appearing in bushes high
Sun rising earlier in the sky
People out walking in the fresh air
Signs of new life everywhere
Chicks start to chirp, birds start to sing
Reminding us what spring has to bring
Lambs skip around, eggs crack in the nest
Spring has arrived, winter gone to rest.

Leah Ewart (10)
The Cope Primary School

My Naughty Little Sister

My naughty little sister jumps up on my bed,
Never thinks of me as she climbs above my head.
She shouts, 'Wakey, wakey, rise and shine,
Come on and play we've got loads of time!'

My naughty little sister never thinks of me
I'm tired and sleepy still
'Go away!' I shout, 'it's Saturday
It's my time to rest, your time to play.'

Good little sister creeps out quietly
Without making any noise,
She closes the door gently
It's back to sleep for me!

Natasha Frizzell (11)
The Cope Primary School

My Naughty Little Brother

I have a naughty brother
He drives me up the wall
Jumps on my head
Thinks he knows it all
Asking me to play
Or read him a book.

He does funny faces
To make us go berserk
Stealing fridge magnets
Throwing them on the floor
Shouts loudly
Sleeps quietly.

Lynsey Browne (10)
The Cope Primary School

Night And Day

Night is so black
With shooting stars in the sky
The moon shining bright
Night is such a beautiful sight
Day is so light
Inviting me to come out and play
'Come out and play' he'd say each day
Then day turns into night
While it turns into night we watch the sunset go down,
It's such a beautiful sight.

Judith Topley (8)
The Cope Primary School

The Famous Rugby Player

He won the World Cup
Can you guess because I can?
He is the world's best kicker,
Well I think he is,
I'll tell you his name . . .
Jonny Wilkinson - my hero!

Matthew Hooks (8)
The Cope Primary School

Where Jesus Lives

You can't catch a plane to take you to Heaven,
Not even a spaceship to get you that far,
You can't get a boat to take you to Heaven,
You can't even go in your daddy's car.

Leanne Wilson (8)
The Cope Primary School

Dolphins

D olphins are exciting!
O ctopuses are great friends to them!
L iving underwater
P robably good for a pet
H appy all the time
I n the sea so blue
N ever hurting you
S plashing everywhere!

Emma Kane (8)
The Cope Primary School

My Puppy Basil

My puppy Basil
Is very jumpy
When it is morning
He is in the garage
If I go to give him breakfast
He jumps up and down
Like a little hyena.

Laura Hewitt (8)
The Cope Primary School

The Sea

The sea shines like a crystal in a cave,
The sea cries when I jump in it,
The great white is fierce,
It lurks about for food
The sea calls me to come every day
But *I'll just miss tea!*

Matthew Irwin (7)
The Cope Primary School

Hockey

Playing hockey is excellent fun
Whoosh flies the puck
'Goal!' We shout.
When I play I imagine I'm at a world championship.
I love to play hockey
Some day I'd like to be a
Professional!

Kerri Hewitt (8)
The Cope Primary School

Giraffes

Giraffes' necks are long,
Into the sky they stretch,
Really high,
A giraffe is brown and yellow,
Free to run,
Free to eat,
Everything they can reach.

Jonathan Hewitt (8)
The Cope Primary School

Clouds

Clouds are very fluffy
They feel like cotton wool,
When they suck up water,
They get very, very full
They drift across the sky,
Like a peaceful gliding swan,
Dripping their shiny diamonds
On my lawn.

Edith Henry (7)
The Cope Primary School

Friends

F riends are loyal and friendship never ends,
R eally good friends never let you down
I n sad and happy times
E veryone plays together
N ever nasty friends
D elight in each other's company
S ometimes fall out but get together soon.

Megan Frizzell (7)
The Cope Primary School

Winter

W inter is a time of year,
I ndoors we stay most of the day
N ot allowed outside to play
T rees are bare and it is grey
E very day I wish the weather will get nice
R eally cold is the snow and ice.

Simon Emerson (8)
The Cope Primary School

Horses

H orses are cute and so are you
O ften they are the loveliest pet you can imagine
R un like the wind they do
S norting and blowing slobbers
E very time they get excited.

Jemma McHugh (7)
The Cope Primary School

The Trip To The Zoo

One day I went to the zoo
And my dad said, 'Oh please go to the kangaroos.'
We went to them, I stuck my thumb in the cage,
It nearly bit my thumb off.
I cried out loud,
'Oh please can we go home instead?'
My dad said, 'Don't worry son,
I'll look after that thumb.'
I kept rhyming on and on
And eventually we got home instead.

Alex Henderson (8)
The Cope Primary School

Horses

Horses in the field jumping, playing
Eating meal and hay
Drinking their water
They love to gallop and kick
Free as the wind.

Alistair Scott (8)
The Cope Primary School

Horses

I love horses
Black, brown, grey and white too.
I like seeing them running free.
They neigh as I pass by.

Samantha Cummings (7)
The Cope Primary School

I'm Not Scared

Now it is night-time
And I go to sleep.
I need to put out the light
So the light is out
And I am sleeping
Snug up in bed
What is that shadow?
'I'm not scared!'

What is that tap tapping on the window?
'I'm not scared!'
What is that face?
'I'm terrified!'

Aaron Winter (8)
The Cope Primary School

Ben

Football lover
English crazy
Funny smiler
Long haired
Big face
Good friend
Constant talker
Maths wizard
Excellent reader.

Adam West (11)
The Cope Primary School

An Enormous Man

An enormous man
Lived with a cat
It was very, very fat
It slept beside a tiny rat
They all lived together
In a teeny, tiny flat.

Rosie Armstrong (7)
The Cope Primary School

My Mum

Here's my mum
She's cross as a bear
She sometimes thinks
That I don't care
But I'll love her
For ever.

Alana McMinn (9)
The Cope Primary School

Eeyore

Eeyore is a friend of mine,
Who didn't know the time!
Was it 1969?
He was not glad
It got really bad
And now he is so sad.

Abigail Duke (10)
The Cope Primary School

Amazing Rocket

The rocket is . . . going . . . going . . . going . . .
Down . . . down . . . down . . .
Bang! It's crashed!
A rocket smells of smoke
When it's launched it has a point
That would give you a poke,
And an astronaut inside I wonder . . .
Could I be an astronaut?

Claire Martin (9)
The Cope Primary School

Boys Vs Girls

Boys are just mad about football.
Boys can look at their hair for hours
Boys drink milk too fast and then be sick.

Girls are smarter than boys
Girls do not look at their hair for hours
Let's just face it, girls are the *best!*

Lynn Brownlee (10)
The Cope Primary School

Aliens

Aliens are so fun
And by the way I am one!
Welcome to my world
And it is curled
Please leave me so I can play
Or I won't have a good day!

Keith Walker (9)
The Cope Primary School

My Family

My family always shout high and low
Everywhere they go,
At my granny's house
My auntie's houses
My mum shouts 'Clean your bedroom,
Or downstairs now.'
So I wrote this poem about them
Because they always shout.
I hate it, I hate it, I hate it, I hate it when they
Shout!

Jennifer West (10)
The Cope Primary School

Apples

Apples are a red sunset
Going into your mouth.
An apple is a juicy, crunchy fruit,
So ripe, so juicy, so yummy.
I have an apple tree so red and ripe
And good for your bones.

Mark Lavery (9)
The Cope Primary School

Camels

Camels are tall and big,
Not small,
They live in deserts and they walk
On the sand,
They are great animals!

Julie Kane (10)
The Cope Primary School

Horse

I love horses
'Cause they are brilliant
But I'm not allowed a horse.
I would like to ride one
'Cause they are brill!
My cousin had a horse
That is why I love horses.
Horses eat mail, grass and hay.

Emma Allen (9)
The Cope Primary School

The Haunted Bus

The bus is dark and gloomy
It's haunted and no one ever
Sits at the back because they blur
Will take whoever it wants.
A boy went down and
Never came back again.
I found a note
It said 'Help!'

Stuart Walker (9)
The Cope Primary School

Boys Are Bad

Girls are good, boys are bad
Girls play good things
Boys play bad
Girls are good, boys are bad
Boys play football
Boys are bad!

Hazel Irwin (10)
The Cope Primary School

My Little Boat

I'll sail across the ocean
In my lovely little boat
The waves will be crashing
Crashing loud.
The wind will be whooshing, howling,
I will be the captain
When the day is right
Sailing, sailing,
Over the sea.

Roger Allen (9)
The Cope Primary School

Donuts

Donuts are my favourite food,
Even when I'm sick of them.
The luscious taste of the icing
And the chocolate sprinkles make
My mouth water.
Yum, those donuts.

Neill Buckley (9)
The Cope Primary School

Cars

Some cars are rusty
Some cars are new
Some cars are old
Some cars are blue
And some cars are
Even made in
Peru!

Rachel McKinney (10)
The Cope Primary School

Safety First

Look to the left,
Look to the right,
Is there a van
Or a motor in sight?
Yes, I can see
A bus and a car.

Then we had better
All stay where we are.
Look to the left,
Look to the right,
Now is there anything
Coming in sight?

Left there is nothing,
Right there is nothing,
Both ways are clear,
Over we cross to the other side.

James Scott (9)
The Cope Primary School

A Boy Who Wanted A Pet

There was a boy
Who wanted a pet
But not an ordinary pet.
He wanted a long nosed pet
That looked like a dog
With quite a long tail
He wants an . . .
Aardvark!
And that's the tale
Of a boy who wanted an aardvark.

Megan Emerson (10)
The Cope Primary School

What People Think About School

Some people think school is a torture house,
Adults must think you just go there to get hit,
But I don't know what I think . . .
Some pupils sing,
Hi-ho Hi-ho
Off to school we go,
We work all day we get no play
Hi-ho Hi-ho Hi-ho.

Some schools have nasty teachers
With a pointy nose with sharp teeth,
I don't blame pupils fainting.
Some people say it is a waste of time,
I think it is alright,
But I don't love it!

Lewis Forsythe (10)
The Cope Primary School

Football!

At the football match
The crowd was very loud
All the players were very proud
Later on the sun shone
At the end the score was 1-0 to Liverpool.

Gareth Strain (10)
The Cope Primary School

Sheep

Fluffy clouds
In the field
They always give us
Wool.

David Bell (10)
The Cope Primary School

Watch Your Back

London City crowded with busy people
Taking the bus.
One bus going to Buckingham Palace was
Invaded by aliens,
(Bad drivers)
Disturbed the Queen at tea,
The guard seized and got zapped
And the Queen was a hostage
And never found!

Daniel Huey (9)
The Cope Primary School

My Little Puppy

I have a puppy
That is very, very cute
He can turn around
And touch the ground.
He can jump high
And reach the sky.
He can chase the bees
Until he falls on his knees.
He can run after mice
Until he turns to ice.

Heather Irwin (9)
The Cope Primary School

Lunchtime

Ding-dong goes the bell,
It's time for lunch said Miss Kell,
Eating sandwiches, sucking juice,
Time is up, back to work!

Robert Winter (9)
The Cope Primary School

Meddling Muddle

'Don't touch that magic spell book'
The wizard warned the boy,
'Just get on with the sweeping,
I'm off to see King Roy.'
The wizard left the workshop
The boy ran up the stairs,
He rummaged through the bookcase
And found the spell book there.
He turned the pages quickly
To find the brushing spell,
He chanted all the verses
He thought that all was well,
Then he started shrinking
He got an awful fright,
He cast the spell so quickly
He hadn't said it right.
The wizard came back later
He peered around the door
The boy had disappeared
And a mouse was on the floor.
'You foolish little creature
You meddle with my book,
I have to turn you back again
Now let me have a look.'
There was a bolt of lightning
And the boy stood there again
'Now let that be a lesson,'
The wizard's voice was cold.
'Never play with magic
And do as you are *told!*'

Carrie Wright (11)
The Cope Primary School